T0209076

UNDERSTAND

Marine Sergeant Michael Secli's journey from the streets of Hell's Kitchen to the hell of Khe Sanh

JERRY F. LIMONE

With
Michael Secli

authorHOUSE®

AuthorHouse™
1663 Liberty Drive
Bloomington, IN 47403
www.authorhouse.com
Phone: 833-262-8899

Published by AuthorHouse 12/13/2022

ISBN: 978-1-6655-7770-0 (sc)
ISBN: 978-1-6655-7771-7 (e)

Library of Congress Control Number: 2022922817

Print information available on the last page.

Front Cover Credits to Michael Secli after one of many battles at Khe Sanh.
Back Cover: Photo of Secli's service uniform which actual
uniform is exhibited along with the front cover photo at the
National Marine Museum in Triangle, Virginia.

This book is printed on acid-free paper.

DEDICATION

To all those who have given part of their own lives and those who gave all to serve their country and fellow citizens with honor and integrity.

THANK YOU

Special thanks to Craig W Tourte, Khe Sanh Veterans Association Board Secretary, for his help in establishing important character references and time lines.

Michael Secli on the left with Craig Tourte, Okinawa 1967

CONTENTS

FOREWORD

How does one capture lightening in a bottle? It seems like a crazy idea. To take something as powerful as lightening, contain it, control it and use it flies in the face of reality. Yet it is known that lightening is a powerful natural force that creates unbelievable energy and often unbelievable destruction. Some day that energy will be harnessed without the accompanying destruction.

This can be said about human beings whose energy can come in the way of intelligence, creativity and motivation. This is the lightening that each person has at their command when they learn how to access it. There is power waiting to be exercised. Once that energy is controlled and applied positively both the giver and the receiver are raised up.

While it is no simple task to control the destructive part of human nature, it can be done, and many have succeeded. It takes a concentrated effort and willingness to make the best of the gifts each person has. Often it takes time to recognize the potential energy and separate the destructive part from the gift giving power that attracts and benefits those in its presence. Some discover this power early in life and for others it comes later. Unfortunately, there are those that never learn to use this force for good. The power is there and the choice to use it is there as well.

Through a lifetime of challenges, it seemed the spark that could unleash the energy was always there for Michael Secli. Always there was a sense of fairness, goodness and loyalty, but often the energy would explode into violence or disruptive actions. He wasn't tapped into the energy. It was there and helped him overcome obstacles, but sometimes the method would get in the way.

There is no formula that explains when and how this conversion takes place. It is different for each person but is clearly recognizable when it happens. There is a magnetism that draws others, makes them smile and want to be part of that universe. It's as if someone said to them, "Sit down with me. Tell me more. Let me be part of what is bubbling out of you."

The beauty of the conversion is that people are attracted by this irresistible force. Lightening in a bottle? Actually, it is lightening's force released from the bottle so others can gain energy from the positive power that is transferred.

Will you become that person? You are your own person that now sees the way to capitalize on the gifts and talents that are unique to you. Power has been transferred that it can now be passed along through your individual style.

As Michael's youngest son, Cameron has seen this in his father and expressed how he felt in a note to his father after having read the original manuscript for this book.

> "Just wanted to say also last night I feel I didn't properly tell you what I wanted to tell you. Not only being my father, I always thought you were my hero. Just looking at you as a man, you are sharp, smart and the definition of hard core. You are always someone I can strive to be. You are a born leader regardless of the Marines. It is an honor and blessing that I am your son and can call you my father and friend.
>
> Love you my pal"

Michael provided the lightening, the electricity that turned on the light in his son. Now his son can go forward in his own way to share that gift with others. The power is there, it needs to be activated so others can have that feeling. What a glorious responsibility.

INTRODUCTION

It was the fall of 2019 when I met Michael Secli. It was a time in my life when I wasn't looking for or expecting to find a new friend. My tendency is to be somewhat reserved socially. I had some good old and dear friends, but at seventy-five years old I had lost some of those and others had moved away. I had plenty of acquaintances, but a real friend was not something I expected. Life has a way of moving things in unexpected directions.

I was being treated for a prostate condition that required eight weeks of radiation treatments, five days a week for eight weeks. What a drag! First, I would check in with the receptionist for my appointment and then I was sent to a waiting area where I would be called in to the next room for my treatment. There were two chairs in the treatment area, one for the next patient and the other chair for the following patient. For whatever series of coincidences, it was usually Michael or me in one of those chairs. Crazy way to meet a friend, but here was a man that seemed to fill up a room with his personality. Every receptionist, nurse, doctor or technician lit up like a Christmas tree when he came into the room. I had to know more about him.

As the weeks passed, I did learn more about this man, his family and his service to our country as a Marine. From my experience with people who served in armed conflicts, most were not willing to talk about it. There are deep reasons for this that as a layman I cannot fully understand and to speculate never seemed to do justice to such suffering. But Michael was different, and it just seemed that there was a smooth flow from one event to another. That's when I mentioned to Michael that other people needed to hear what he had to say.

The mid 1960's to the mid 1970's were troubling times for our country; from assassinations to a war and the trying of a President. The War in Viet Nam was not popular (as if any war is popular) for a long time. It seemed those who served were not welcomed home as heroes and worse were reviled by many whom these men and women believed they were defending. It is difficult to understand how Michael Secli was able to light up a room in 2019.

Understanding is a tricky thing. The most simplistic form of understanding is when a series of facts are presented, and a conclusion can be drawn from those facts. Science is like that. We understand that one plus one equals two. Understanding human behavior goes outside the bounds of simple cause and effect. In Michael's case, if one plus one equaled two he should have been a bitter resentful man crippled by his experience, but not Michael. Why?

I am sure there is an explanation somewhere. Understanding how Michael got to be where he is today, takes more than science. It takes compassion, a willingness to see what is good and how often good can come from what is seemingly awful and evil.

CHAPTER 1

BABY KILLER

It was mid-April 1968, when the 1st Battalion Twenty-sixth Marines (reinforced) and nineteen year-old Michael Secli of the Thirteenth Marines were being transported to a base in Da Nang Vietnam. This was after having served seventy-seven straight days, from January 20th to April 1st, 1968, defending the Khe Sanh combat base. Through monsoon weather and enemy forces that far outnumbered them, they had held their ground and denied the enemy any military or psychological victory. It was time for these men to find some rest.

It was still Vietnam, but Da Nang seemed a world apart after seventy-seven days of deprivation. There were warm showers to wash away the red dirt that seemed to be embedded in every inch of their skin, soap that smelled good, warm socks and toilet paper. Amazing what could seem like heaven after being through hell.

It would take more than one shower to remove that red dirt and the stench of combat, but Michael was alive and there was a lightness that was present among these men who had faced death on a daily basis. Much of the military formality was set aside as there was more joking among the ranks and less saluting. This atmosphere was understood and appreciated by combat veterans of all ranks. There was the occasional commissioned officer, new to circumstances such as these, that were put off by not being saluted or accorded the traditional respect of rank. In some cases they were reminded by their superiors why these circumstances called for a different decorum.

It was time for Michael to prepare for a trip to Okinawa, Japan, where he would take part in what was called an evaluation. As he stood out in the airfield awaiting a military transport on Saturn Airlines, he could feel the heat and dust weighted down by moisture pressing in on him. All this would be left behind. There was a mixture of somberness and joy heightened by the individual fighter jets taking off and their pilots giving a 'thumbs up' sign to those preparing to leave.

Michael thought, "Yes I'm going home but….."

There was an uncertainty jumbled up with joy and anxiety.

"I was alive and looking forward to seeing the people that for so long had been the center of my life, yet somehow the war had changed me in ways that I couldn't explain to anyone, never mind myself."

Being happy and fearful at the same time was the closest he could come to explaining this feeling.

Everything was quiet and still as they boarded the plane to Okinawa. At the same time there was an aura of tightness or tenseness among those on board. Perhaps it was the idea that all still remained in Vietnam and this would not be real until they left the ground.

Sure enough as the plane left the ground, a universal cheer went up and the tension was broken. Chatter continued amongst the Marines until they landed in Okinawa.

"Evaluation", Michael said, "That's what they called it. They wanted to see if we would be fit to return to a world that would never seem the same to us."

There were some among the group being evaluated that appeared the doctors thought needed more treatment in Okinawa before they were in any condition to return to the states. This was a whole new experience for Michael and as he heard of the men being evaluated speak to the doctors and other soldiers, he thought, "Some of these guys are crazy. In effect we all had to be crazy to do this job. Where was the line between who was crazy and who was going home. What I did know was that I was going home."

Maybe the difference between crazy and going home was that Michael came from a home in the first place.

"When my evaluation week was completed, an American Airlines flight was assigned to take me, another Marine and two servicemen from the Army for the first leg of our trip to Anchorage, Alaska and then on to San Diego, California."

It was fitting that Michael had three other comrades in arms with which to travel, for only those who experience combat can truly relate to another veteran exposed to the violence of war. That experience might be equated to being a living part of 'Dante's Inferno'. While never descending to eighth and ninth levels of fraud and deceit, but living within those circles, dealing with an enemy that at times appeared to be a friend and at once could become a death sentence was when the need for people you could trust and count on was everything.

"What I knew was that these men sitting beside me would never leave me behind on the battlefield or any time I needed someone to stand by my side".

It is probably the reason why those with military relationships consider such relationships as more than friends. They were buddies for life!

The flight from Okinawa to San Diego seemed like a dream. There were memories and contemplations that seemed to flow like water down a rocky stream. It was like time had vanished as if the waters escorted Michael through time.

"Before I could think about it, we were on the ground."

The plane taxied and settled into its spot on the tarmac and passenger ladders were rolled into place so passengers could disembark and walk from there to the nearby terminal. Michael and his three buddies set out with the rest of the passengers.

"As the four of us headed for the terminal a loud report rang out as if a gun was fired or a bomb exploded. We couldn't tell what it was."

For that minute the men were back in Vietnam and under enemy fire. They dove to the ground with shouts of, "Hit the deck; in coming!" As it turned out it was only the four warriors that were on the ground. It sounded like enemy fire, but it was one of the vehicles tugging the luggage carts that had backfired.

"In our minds we were still in a war zone."

Some might say this was 'shell shock' or PTSD or whatever else psychology decided to call it; they were living it. It didn't go away just because they were in the 'safety' of their home country.

Michael looked around, "When we got to our feet, dusted ourselves off and with embarrassed smiles headed toward our connecting flights, I realized I had torn a hole in one of the legs of my dress uniform. I didn't like the look of it and combined with the fact that the incident also left the rest of my uniform dusty and disheveled; what was I to do? I couldn't fix the rip in my trousers, but I got to the men's room and straightened myself out as best I could, making sure my shirt was properly bloused and jacket and pants neatly brushed."

The operators of the luggage carts were horrified and frightened by the scene they had created; however they had the dignity to apologize and contact their superiors at American Airlines. The chain didn't stop there. Their superiors relayed the event to the nearest Marine headquarters. It wasn't long after when a Marine Lance Corporal arrived.

Michael was stunned, "To my amazement the lance corporal began to take measurements for a new uniform and in addition a new pair of uniform shoes."

Through the whirlwind of activity Michael lost track of time and realized that his connecting flight had departed.

"It occurred to me that my father, my uncles and Dad's best friend would be expecting my arrival to Kennedy Airport at the original time. I was able to reach them at home well before they would have to leave for the airport to meet me at the original time. I let them know that everything was fine and while I would be delayed, American Airlines got me on their next flight into Kennedy."

It seemed like everything was moving at warp speed. One minute Michael was being measured and the next minute the uniform was there. The next second the uniform was on and the next minute he was on his new connecting flight.

"What happened here," Michael thought.

All these events one after the other in rapid succession left Michael in a state of suspended animation.

"I got lost in my thoughts with all I had gone through up until that point and the excitement of going home that it seemed like only minutes when I heard the pilot telling us to prepare for the approach to Kennedy Airport."

As the plane made its approach coming home no longer seemed like an abstract dream. The landmarks around the city confirmed this wasn't a dream. This was home.

The plane taxied into the gate and this time there was no drama involving sounds that could be mistaken for enemy fire. This time the drama was seeing family for the first time in over a year and that once again they could be part of a life that Michael had been blessed to have the privilege to live. As Michael disembarked there was an area where those waiting for passengers were assembled.

"it seemed like I was looking down a long corridor where in the distance I could faintly see my father, two uncles, Frankie and Nicky, and Mandy, my father's best friend."

Michael was overcome with emotions which words could not adequately describe. There was ecstatic happiness that was almost paralyzing mixed with relief and an overwhelming sense of protective love that could not be spoken or explained

Michael's father spoke the first words, "My son."

Michael finally found his voice saying, "I'm home."

As was their custom Michael's father hugged him and gave him a kiss on the cheek. While they both struggled for words and being overwhelmed by emotion, Michael's father asked, "What do you want?"

Michael thought, "If my mother was here she would have asked, Michael can I get you something to eat?"

But Mom wasn't there, so the two of them had to work through their emotions in their own way.

Michael's father broke the silence, "Let's go home."

With those simple words and the physical show of affection, it was all that was needed. It was the beginning of a memorable evening as Michael got into the car with Uncle Frankie driving and Uncle Nicky sitting with him up front. Michael sat in the back between his father and Mandy.

Michael recollected how the rest of the evening got started.

"Uncle Frankie and Nicky drove us from the airport and dropped my father, Mandy and me at the bowling alley bar on the corner next to the Port Authority Bus Terminal. I suggested we have a drink to celebrate my homecoming."

Michael's father was very proud of his son and wanted to share this day of good fortune with his friends before heading home. What better way to do it than with his best friend Mandy and another long time friend who was the bartender. There was a sense of camaraderie shared amongst bartenders making this very important to Michael's father.

"My father owned a bar in the neighborhood and these two men would often come into the other man's establishment, have a drink, and leave a crazy big tip as a sign of respect."

Michael and his father had a custom going back to early Thanksgiving days of sharing a scotch sour to celebrate. While it wasn't Thanksgiving on the calendar there were certainly enough thanks to celebrate. When they finished their drinks, Michael's father left a twenty dollar tip.

Michael was shocked by the size of tip and commented in a hushed voice, "Dad this is way too much!"

At that point Michael's father 'educated' him on the custom of respect.

The three of them left the bar and crossed to 40th Street and Ninth Avenue where Michael's father grew up. Across the street was Saint Clemens Mary where Michael went to school.

As they talked and reminisced, all of a sudden as if out of nowhere, a man jumped in front of Michael.

Maybe it was his military training, but Michael could feel something coming.

"I sensed there was someone coming at me, so in my way I was prepared."

The man shouted in Michael's face, "Baby Killer!"

In that instant the attacker flipped up Michael's service medals which started to fall to the ground. In Michael's mind it was almost like slow motion.

"I knew he was there and before the medals had a chance to hit the ground, I had the man on his back, the medals fluttering onto the attacker's chest, an enemy to be dealt with."

Fortunately a cop came along just in time, rapping the assailant in his ribs and ordering him to get up and asking Michael, "Do you want to press charges?"

"I just wanted to get out of there and had no interest in pressing chargers. I was grateful the police officer came before more serious damage had occurred. If that officer hadn't come the attacker would never have gotten off the ground. I was trained to kill the enemy."

It was a young man, not much older than Michael, who had no idea what kind of a person Michael was and what his role was as a Marine, but he saw the uniform and maybe heard stories about people in the war who killed young children.

"Not only did he attack me physically, but he attacked my integrity as a Marine and a person sworn to defend him."

Once again, Michael had to get himself cleaned up and looking like the sharp disciplined Marine he was so proud to be.

Why did he still have to fight the war? Would he ever be left to enjoy a life like the rest of society?

After getting cleaned up Michael came back out to the street and the police officer was still there and wanted to know if Michael was alright.

"Yes", he said, "I'm fine."

Michael's father looked at him and didn't know what to say. Finally, a little while later through a choked up throat he said, "Glad you're home son."

Mandy was totally overwhelmed by the experience and what he saw in Michael's eyes that day. They were eyes filled with blood like some demon from another world forced to do battle. It was not just the blood in his eyes, but the otherness of facial expression and bodily response. He was trained to kill when attacked.

"Neither Mandy nor my father had ever seen anything like that in me or any other man. Everything had changed."

In order for everyone to calm down, Michael's father decided they should stop at J&J Bar on 39th Street off of Ninth Avenue. This was Hell's Kitchen and the bar was a hangout for some of the toughest guys in the neighborhood. From gangs to those who were connected, it was not a place for tourists. But it was their neighborhood.

Despite this reputation, after Michael's father related the story of what just transpired and what they saw in Michael's demeanor, a quiet tension came over those who were in the bar. This was not the same seventeen or eighteen year-old boy who used to park cars at J&J.

The tension grew thicker when two strangers wandered into the bar exhibiting a bravado and arrogance that normally had no place among those who frequented J&J's. They walked into a place that had all the signs of an explosion ready to take place. This was not the time for them or any other person to add to the existing tension. The owner was in no mood for an explosive confrontation and made that known to the intruders. They were asked to leave and finally had to be escorted out to avoid any problems.

"Even in the J&J Bar I was feared or there was a fear I might erupt in anger or defense. Was I home? It was no longer the home I knew when I left. Everything seemed to have changed."

How did all this get started?

CHAPTER 2

THE NEIGHBORHOOD

On the surface it is never really known what causes a person's actions and behavior. For the most part who knows what makes people think and act as they do. Humans are complicated entities pushed by forces that are sometimes unknown and often unseen. People become the victims and the beneficiaries in relation to all that is seen and unseen, known and unknown. Perhaps the most influential factors, beyond family, are the time and place within which one grows.

For Michael, the time started in the 1950's as the country rolled through the post World War II period. Coming off the great wartime victory, patriotism was at its height. People were proud of their country and the flag that stood for the sacrifices made by the heroes that kept the world free.

It wasn't perfect, nothing ever is. The country was experiencing tremendous economic growth as manufacturing and construction were reaching levels never experienced before. It was all part of the post-World War ll economic expansion. Along with this growth, the country as a whole tended to be socially conservative. However, now that there was more opportunity and more money for a large segment of the population, materialism crept into the psyche of the country. Those who were not part of this rising availability of opportunity and money sought to attain what they could through whatever means available to them.

During the presidency of Harry S. Truman, the Korean War entered into this mix and lasted from June 25, 1950 until it ended in a bloody stalemate on July 27, 1953. The country was not use to a war that couldn't be won. It was the beginning of such wars to stop the spread of Communism. During this time the Cold War between the Western World led by the United States and the USSR as the enemies, reached levels that created both fear of physical extinction and psychological fear generated by the specter of Communism. This fear was brought to its apex with the McCarthy hearings. Led by Joseph McCarthy in 1950, over 200 people in the State Department were said to have been infiltrated by Communists. After McCarthy was elected to Congress in 1952, he proceeded with anti communist investigations none of which were ever substantiated. Never-the-less his aggressive tactics led to the persecution and the loss of livelihood of many innocent people.

January 20, 1953, retired general Dwight D Eisenhower was elected president, serving two terms until January 20, 1961. During that time he notably expanded social security, helped establish the interstate highway system and entered into the 'space race' after the launch of Sputnik 1 in 1957. He then signed The National Defense Education Act leading to the creation of NASA.

The 1950's were the precursor to the civil rights movements in the 60's. It began with the Supreme Court ruling of 1954 Brown vs the Board of Education in which all Americans were guaranteed a fair education regardless of race, creed or religion. In keeping with this ruling, The Little Rock Nine in 1957 integrated the Little Rock Central High School which was a key to the hope of ending segregation in schools and other public places. This was the beginning of laws and actions to promote equal treatment of Black Americans. As history has shown, laws did not always lead to the desired results no matter the view.

It was during this time that Michael's life began its formation in a place called Hell's Kitchen. This was an area in New York's Manhattan borough that in those days stretched from 34th Street to 57th Street west of 8th Avenue to the Hudson River. No one is exactly sure how the name originated as some accounts go all the way back as far as 1835 when Davy Crockett gave his assessment after having visited the area, saying "In my part of the country, when you meet an Irishman, you find a first rate gentleman; but these are worse than savages; they are too mean to swab Hell's kitchen."[1] All the naming seems to stem from the area around 39th

Street. In September of 1881 a New York Times reporter was investigating a multiple murder in the West 30's and referred to a filthy tenement on 39th Street and 10th Avenue as "Hell's Kitchen", saying it was "probably the lowest and filthiest place in the city."[2] Then again in the early Twentieth Century there is the story of Dutch Fred the Cop who was a veteran officer watching a riot on West 39th Street near 10th Avenue with his rookie partner who commented, "This place is hell itself." To which Fred responded, "Hell's a mild climate. This is Hell's Kitchen."[3] As all these stories indicated, it was a rough and tumble area where one had to be tough to survive and often had to aid that survival by doing what some might consider at worst illegal and at best questionable.

While Michael was born November 15, 1946, it was the 1950's where his formation as a person began. The area still was rough and tumble with gangs and gangsters of every kind. So much so that it even inspired the great musical, West Side Story by Leonard Bernstein which debuted on September 26, 1957, giving a sliver of an idea what the area held for Michael. One had to grow up tough to survive and creative to thrive.

For Michael, the part of Hell's Kitchen where he grew up was a tight knit community of mostly first and second generation Italian immigrants. They were poor people who struggled to survive in a hostile environment beyond their neighborhood. It was the family ties along with valued friends that made survival more manageable and at times fun and entertaining.

Michael's family lived in a three room flat with four people including Michael and his sister Donna, along with his father Menatti and his mother Angelina. It was a three room flat for four people and a bathroom that they had to share with a neighbor. Upstairs on the fifth floor was where his grandparents lived. Their living conditions included two apartments that took up the entire floor, so they had their own bathroom befitting the respect given to those who had earned this convenience from years of hard fought battles. While this 'luxury' of a private bathroom was hard won, there was no escaping the fact that refrigeration consisted of an icebox which all the tenants waited for their block of ice that were regularly scheduled to maintain the contents of the icebox.

Yes, they were poor, but with family and friends they managed. There was the Children's Aid Society that at the age of four in 1950, Michael got to go to a summer camp in upstate New York. Charity was a ticket out of Hell's Kitchen for a few weeks in the summer. This only lasted for two more years until Michael was six years old in 1953. There was only this little window of time where a child could be carefree for a few weeks, then the reality of Hell's Kitchen would be the center of life. Yes, the fun didn't last long in this neighborhood.

As Michael grew up after those early carefree days, he started to attend school at Saint Clemens Mary that was associated with the Children's Aid Society. He would attend school there through the eighth grade. If being a practicing Catholic meant going to church every

Sunday, Michael's family did not hold that mantel. But Michael attended Saint Clemens Mary where this close-knit community found refuge from an outside world that threatened their way of life and seemed to disrupt and interfere with their traditions. They created their own community and their own customs and to a point, their own laws.

There was a hierarchy that was based upon respect for those who had made their reputation as the expression goes, 'by hook or by crook.' One never knew where the connections ended, but one always knew where they stood in the line of connections

During this time, Menatti, Michael's father, was best friends with Mandy who lived next door to the church on 40th Street. Mandy worked for a bookie named Nicky. Every bowling night Mandy would go to the alleys dressed in a low-key manner that made a point about his position and that he was there for business. Nicky was a flashy dresser, and he apparently attracted attention to bring in the customers. Nicky was not the end connection because he had to report to Tony. Tony had the big volume bookie business and while he was low key in the way he spoke, he also dressed like a regular street guy. His appearance as well as his actions spoke loudly of his status and as a result he was highly respected in the neighborhood and was seen as being well connected.

Surely Tony had to answer to another level, but that level was not known around 39th Street. It was something best not known unless you wished to go down a rabbit hole you might not be prepared to handle and from which you might never return.

Uncle Franky was Menatti Secli's brother-in-law. He held a special place in the family and as such was given the honor and responsibility to be Michael's godfather. Franky was highly respected in the neighborhood and the word on the street was, "Don't fuck with Tarzan." They called Uncle Franky Tarzan because he was a tough guy in charge of stage hands down in the theater district. These were union jobs that were highly sought and often you needed to have a connection to get in. Franky had to be a tough guy to handle the kind of people that might have thought their connections entitled them to special treatment.

Franky was no slouch as a card player, another skill he acquired that added to his reputation. He was married to Lulu, Menatti's sister. The story goes that Franky got into a card game with a man who was running out of money and thought he had the winning cards in his hand. When Franky raised the ante, this man who thought he had the winning cards believed his hand was so good that instead of money he put up his property in Sag Harbor out on the South Shore of Long Island. Franky had the cards and now he had the property in Sag Harbor. It wasn't the Sag Harbor of the 2000's, but still a valuable piece of property. Not bad for a tough guy from Hell's Kitchen.

This was the neighborhood and the environment in which Michael grew up. You took your chances and sometimes you could win big, but there was always the chance that you were on the other end of a losing bet. For him it was somewhat of a protective environment as he approached seventh and eighth grade at Saint Clemens Mary. Michael became an altar boy in the seventh grade, kind of a rite of passage if you attended school at Saint Clemens Mary. This was the ultimate church experience made even more memorable by having a chance to get into the unconsecrated wine that the altar boys prepared for the priest.

This was life until Michael left Saint Clemens Mary grammar school at the end of eighth grade. The year was 1959, when Michael was fourteen years old and would turn fifteen that coming November 15. That fall would mean a new school away from the neighborhood and the usual protections provided by the neighborhood. Michael had learned much about street smarts and how to survive the streets, but was not given the encouragement or the opportunity to turn those street smarts into academic success. So where did that leave him on life's next step on the ladder? Well, if academics were not in the picture it would be learning a trade.

There were no trade schools found in the Hell's Kitchen section of Manhattan. He would have to travel 37 blocks north and eight blocks east to 96th Street between 1st and 2nd Avenue. This was where the Public School for Machine and Metal Trades was located. It later became known as Manhattan Vo. Tech. It was a long way from the home where Michael had grown up. Being so far removed from what had been the center of his life and going to a school that held no interest to him, it became in his mind what he called, "The school for losers."

The first two months at his new school Michael and some friends would stop for coffee and chocolate donuts before school started at a place called Sylvia's. This was unfamiliar territory outside the old neighborhood. There was something in its unfamiliarity outside of his protective neighborhood that held the lurking threat of danger. Michael could feel it, sense it and so it started.

There was a black student going to Michael's new school who by appearance seemed much older than Michael. His name was Griffin and to Michael's young and inexperienced eyes seemed more like an adult than a student, with lips that appeared to be large, a nose that looked flattened and hair cropped so short he almost looked bald headed. In Michael's eyes he appeared as an instant threat. He would observe Michael and his friends every morning as they ordered their coffee and chocolate donuts. He was a bully and wanted to make sure Michael understood that this was his territory and that he was the law in this part of town.

The first time Griffin came into Sylvia's he stood behind Michael and started to grab for Michael's donut. As Griffin reached over to grab the donut Michael said, "Who the hell do you think you are? You're not taking what belongs to me." Griffin did not take the donut but said, "We'll see about that!"

The next morning at Sylvia's Griffin came in again, but this time he had three of his gang waiting outside to see what Michael would do. Michael was not about to get into a situation where he was outnumbered by people looking to make an example of him and prove whose territory this was. The street smarts kicked in. He let the donut go. It was the beginning of the terrorism that led to Griffin demanding two dollars each week as protection money. Two dollars in 1959 was likely half of what Michael had for the week, not to mention the humility of being a victim of another individual.

Michael's friend B.J., Bobby Jennings asked Michael, "What are you going to do." Michael turned in anger, spitting out the words, "Well he is not getting two dollars a week from me!"

Michael hatched a plan. He would tell Griffin where to meet him so he could start paying according to Griffin's demands. He started by saying, I don't have money with me now, but if you meet me tomorrow before school starts down by the janitor's office I'll have the money for you."

Michael got there to the spot they agreed upon the next morning. He was there well before the time that Griffin was to show. Michael needed to make sure everything was in order in case Griffin came with some of his gang. He brought with him a thin metal club like weapon that when swung its length would increase. This allowed for it to be concealed, but still to be extended allowing for more force while keeping his distance. He waited with his back against the door to the janitor's office so if Griffin did bring friends they would be unable to get behind him. At the designated time Griffin arrived to collect his extortion money. It was just Griffin; no gang members. Michael felt a little sense of relief, knowing that he only had to deal with Griffin.

As Griffin approached Michael he called out in a derisive tone, "All right you little mother fucker let's get started. Hand over your first installment." Michael pretended to reach into his pocket for the money and instead brought around the metal club that made a ringing sound as it extended to its full length before striking Griffin across the face causing a bloody gash from his left ear, across his left cheek, over his left jaw down to his neck. As his tormentor started to sink to the ground Michael knew that he had to finish the job or become the victim himself. Quickly he gave a blow to the back of the neck that put Griffin prostrate on the floor. With Griffin sprawled on the floor in a pool of blood, Michael finished him off with an angry, hateful, gruesome kick to the face. While this was not generally part of Michael's personality, he had been forced into a defensive position and in the heat of battle with adrenalin running high, thoughts of mercy were shrouded over.

That battle was over as was any chance that Michael would survive if he came back to school. These were tough times as everybody battled for their place and the right to control the territory they saw as their own. That piece of property was not something Michael had any desire to be part of. He didn't like the school to start off with so there was no further need to be part of it.

Michael would soon be fifteen years old with school not being part of his future what could he do? Go back to the neighborhood and work out a new plan? It just seemed like each new plan; each new phase had its own set of roadblocks. Michael was entering early adulthood with all the accompanying adult decision making responsibilities and none of the experience needed to make informed decisions. But this was Hell's Kitchen in the late 50's and you had to grow up fast here; the environment demanded it. The one thing Michael knew from experience was that there were people in the neighborhood he could count on for help. What kind of help?

Back in the neighborhood there was always a way to work the hustle and make a few bucks if you were willing to put forth the effort and weren't shy about what had to be done. There were the seasonal opportunities like selling Christmas trees which season would be coming soon, shoveling snow for the shop keepers and Michael new them all and made sure he would be the first one there to offer his services. Michael had been working with the Christmas trees from the time he was a preteen. His connection was Peter Santo who would supply the trees and Michael would set up outside of Uncle Willy's produce stand over on 40th Street and 9th Avenue. It was a rich experience where Michael not only sold the tress, but often delivered them to the customer's apartments. It was here that he met the many diverse personalities that were part of the fabric of Hell's Kitchen in the mid to late 50's. There were the wise guys, the lonely elderly, the pretty girls and yes, the gay man that everybody new was gay, (they were called homos then) but nobody made an issue of it. He had his place in the neighborhood. It was live and let live. Don't ask don't tell.

But the best money came from working for the businesses that were thriving at the time. Whether it was the meat packing industry or the garment center, that's where the real money was. All through the time Michael was attending Saint Clemens Mary in seventh and eighth grade, his Uncle Willy introduced him to the meat markets owned by the Esposito's and the Bosco's. He would make deliveries from their retail shops to people in the neighborhood using his bicycle. This connection really paid off after the fiasco at The Machine and Metal Trades School.

Phil, who worked at Bosco's, saw something in Michael that he liked and felt the kid would be able to handle the rigors involved in the work down in the meat packing district. It would involve hauling huge sides of beef hanging from hooks in cold trucks and getting them into the processing area where once again they needed to be hung on hooks where they would begin the route for the butchering process. It was hard physical work that the then fifteen year old Michael would do one or two days a week. He might get $200 for those one to two days of work, a considerable amount of money at that time. The bonus was the $25 or more of processed meat he would get to take back home each week.

The meat packing plants were further downtown on Gansevoort and 14th Streets. In the warmer months

Michael could take his bike, but in the winter that was a cold and exhausting two way trip. Michael, the ever inventive hustler, would jump on the back of a bus heading down 14th Street enjoying the warmth coming off the engine and saving the bus fare.

This was an important job, not only for Michael, but for his whole family that were struggling at the time. His father was sick and the only other person working at the time was his mother, Angela, who worked at Schrafft's Restaurant. Schrafft's at that time in the mid 1950's was the place to go for a moderately priced lunch or some ice cream dish for the kids out for the day with the family. It was a very popular place for white people with modest incomes. It was a time in the country's history when blacks were discouraged from entering these establishments. Since it was catering to people with modest incomes, what they paid their employees was modest. So what Michael brought to the table was very important during this difficult time.

Michael worked at the Meat packing plant until he was seventeen. The work was tough and it was time for a change. His father was back at work so Michael felt some freedom to make the change. He had known Peter Santo from the time he was a young teen selling Christmas trees. Peter worked in the garment district delivering goods and thought it would be something that Michael had the skills and the smarts to succeed. The only problem was you needed a driver's license and you had to be eighteen to get one. Michael went back to his neighborhood connections to see if the problem could be resolved.

Michael went to Mandy, his father's best friend and Tony who was Mandy's bookie boss. They had connections to a man who could make fake driver's licenses. Michael would need a driver's license in order to execute his next plan. The guys knew a trucking company that delivered goods into the garment center; Dante's Trucking Company over on 38th Street was Michael's next stop on this winding road. He had the fake license and now he was about to get with Dante's Trucking Company. He would be delivering goods into the garment district along with a lot more experienced, tough men most of whom were two and three times is age.

They set Michael up with the newest truck that had a closed body. That seemed like a good deal and a welcoming gesture to the newest and youngest member in the company. After all, a closed truck seemed ideal for deliveries in foul weather. What Michael didn't realize at first was that an open truck could get more goods on it because the garments could be stacked higher. Another lesson on what looked good at first sight, held truths not necessarily visible to the inexperienced and untrained eye. Michael understood he had a lot to learn. He kept his mouth shut and didn't complain. He was learning how the game was played.

Peter Santo, who had worked at Dante's for many years, had the open truck with the longer body. He had the room to stack garments higher along with additional length making for a bigger, more profitable payload. But Michael was happy he still made great money, about $750.00 a week. Back in the late 50's and early 60's that was a substantial income for many adults, never mind a high school drop out with a fake driver's license.

With a little creativity and a pinch of larceny, Michael was able to enhance his income. He paid attention and learned from what he saw and heard from others delivering into the garment district. Sometimes the loaders at the warehouse where the goods were to be picked up would lose count and might miss five items or sometimes more. When Michael, who paid close attention to the counts, saw this he would slip the miscounts under the pile of clothes that were on the bill of lading. He would sign the bill of lading not noting the miscount. When he delivered the goods to the retail shops he would offer the extra goods at a discounted cash price. It was all part of the standard hustle. You might be considered stupid if you weren't part of the hustle. This was the way things were done; an accepted piece of the scramble to survive.

As Michael grew up in this atmosphere there was also some time for doing the fun things in which young teens and maturing teens could take part. Among some of the street games there was stoop ball, stick ball and street hockey. Street hockey became one of Michael's passions. He learned about the best skates that used steel wheels costing fifty cents apiece. It was a high price for a high performance wheel that lasted longer and provided a smoother ride on the rough streets. That in addition to actual skate shoes that were like boots rather than the cheap version that involved using street shoes that slipped into metal skates. These were skates that were like part of the foot and ankle and made all the difference.

Michael and his friends got so good they began to play against competition from across the river in Jersey City and West New York. One of the coaches from the West New York team was so impressed with Michael's play that he encouraged Michael to transfer those skills to ice hockey. Michael really liked the idea, but he found that skating on ice was very different from street hockey. Trying to make turns and keep the ankles from turning over was a big challenge. He was a great New York Ranger fan and wanted very much to learn the skating techniques the pros used.

One day Michael's Uncle Tony, who drove a truck and had a truck route that took him past Madison Square Garden, took Michael with him and dropped him off across the street from the Garden around 50th and 8th Avenue, the location of the Garden before it eventually moved to the new location at 7th Avenue and 31st Street. There was a gift shop dedicated to the Rangers that besides having the customary Ranger shirts and other Ranger gifts also carried high quality equipment, including skates. What he really wanted was a pair of skates that fit properly and could give him that same confidence he had on the street skates.

While looking over the ice skates, out the corner of his eye Michael saw a hulking figure that looked familiar to him. As he turned to face the man, he blurted out, "Hey Lou." It was Lou Fortinato the tough defenseman who played for the Rangers. Lou was a tough guy who was nicknamed 'Leapin' Louie', probably for his tough, aggressive, and close to maniacal play on defense.

The tough guy decided to take Michael under his wing. Lou said, "What's your size kid." After Michael gave him his size, Lou said, "Let's get something a little smaller." "Why", Michael questioned. This really seemed odd. "Well if you want to get the proper support these skates need to fit so tight that they are like a part of your foot."

Lou then took Michael out on the ice for a fifteen minute session to start training him to turn, stop and skate backwards. For several weeks Michael would meet Lou two to three times a week to continue those lessons until Michael could make sharp turns, come to a sudden stop after racing at high speed throwing up a magnificent ice spray and skating backwards like it was second nature. At this point, Michael was ready for competitive ice hockey with the group from West New York across the river. Lou was there for his pupil's first game.

Lou had his professional obligations and was not able to attend other games, but when Michael scored his first goal he wanted to make sure Lou knew of his accomplishment. At the end of the game Michael got the puck with which he scored his first goal, found a box that it fit perfectly into like an expensive piece of jewelry, wrapped and presented it to his mentor. It would be the last time he would see Lou Fortinato as Lou left him saying, "You're going to be alright kid."

Those words would be more prophetic than either of them realized. At seventeen and eighteen years old Michael would earn an MVP award for his skill on the ice and contribution to his team's success as well as a sportsmanship award for his fair play and knowledge of the game. He knew how to take a hit as well as give one, but never needed to resort to unsportsmanlike behavior.

Along with the tough times of growing up in Hell's Kitchen there were some rewards for hard work and dedication. But it seemed like no matter who you were, you were always living on the edge of danger. All the minor and borderline indiscretions often ballooned into something that no one could see or predict.

CHAPTER 3

WALKING AND CROSSING THE LINE

Oh yea, it was great fun hanging out with friends and hustling a few dollars parking cars for customers that drank and socialized at the J&J Bar. Technically, a driver's license was needed to move cars that the customers dropped off, but this was Hell's Kitchen in the early 60's and Michael and many of his friends were at most seventeen and at least a year away from a legal driver's license. Michael had his fake driver's license complements of his neighborhood connections, but none of that mattered; it was the neighborhood and everybody knew the deal, so the adults worked with the teens to get the job done. No harm, no foul. So the law was skirted and nobody got hurt. The game was played by the rules set in the neighborhood.

Where the cars got parked was only two blocks from the bar on 37th and 38th Streets, next to where the Port Authority parked the city buses that also went to and from New Jersey carrying commuters. Outside the bus lot was Frankie DePalma who was supposedly keeping an eye on the lot making sure that the buses were secure. Frankie was a fat, disheveled, borderline homeless man who was more of a local character than a real security presence, so he was no threat to Michael and his street smart friends. They knew that the drivers left the keys in the buses so they could get off to an early start as soon as they arrived for their shift.

In the winter, when it was cold, after having parked the cars for the J&J customers Michael and his friends would walk past Frankie DePalma, get into one of the buses, start the engine and turn up the heat. There they would set up a card game and play cards until the patrons at J&J needed their cars. Comfort and warmth until that time was complements of the Port Authority.

In the same area around 38th Street, was another parking facility for commuter cars or people visiting the city and also for city dwellers that needed a place to safely park their car. Michael and his friends were very familiar with how the parking areas operated. This was New York, 1963, and security measures were nowhere near modern security standards. Being familiar with the parking garage operation it was easy to walk right in to where the cars were parked. There were keys to cars left on a board, but there were keys that were often left with the car. These keys could be found behind the driver's side visor or sometimes sitting on top of a tire in one of the wheel wells. Those were the keys that Michael and his friends would look for. The 'secret' was to pick a car that was not flashy, but rather one that what they called, 'an old man's car', like an old Chrysler with the push button transmission on the dashboard. The car also had to have at least a half tank of gas or they would go on to the next car.

The daring nature of using somebody's car, for the most part somebody you didn't know, and taking it for a joy ride was all part of the thrill. If you asked Michael why he did it, his answer would be, "For the excitement, the kicks!'

The trip usually was to Coney Island, returning late in the evening when the streets were quiet. It could be pretty scary coming in that late because getting lost in the crowd of traffic was no longer an option. With a car load of teenage boys looking too young to drive legally, left them vulnerable to being stopped by the police. It was all good fun, part of the thrill. True, the law was broken, but nobody got hurt so what's the harm?

"We were just having fun, adventure, kicks and hanging together. It was kind of a club and every club needed a clubhouse."

So Michael and his friends, some would call them a gang, saw the ideal spot for a clubhouse. It was an old abandoned tenement behind the J&J Bar, between 38th Street and 9th and 10th avenue with a basement apartment not very visible from the street. Above the basement apartment there was a Mexican family known to Michael and his friends as the Bravos.

"We had more or less of an agreement with the family, actually the matriarch of the family, Senora Bravos, that we would be quiet and not draw attention to what was their 'home'."

The boys were careful not to draw unnecessary attention to the building so it was a rule that no females were to be invited and there would be no parties in the clubhouse. This was to be a place to hang out and make plans for the next adventure whether it be a scheme to make money or a way to get furniture for the clubhouse.

Furniture was a key ingredient for a completed clubhouse. Most things left out on the curb in this neighborhood were beyond being useful. Since there was no money available to buy furniture, options for obtaining something useful were limited. Sometimes opportunities would present themselves at the most unexpected times.

"Actually me and four of my friends were on our way to a get together at a CYO gathering at our local church around 34th Street when we passed a high rise building on 34th Street and 9th Avenue. In the lobby we saw a sofa and a large matching chair. For some reason the doorman was not at his post. It was an opening we couldn't resist. We took the sofa and the chairs and carried them back to the clubhouse."

Needless to say, they never made it to the CYO gathering. It was a world of contradictions if one was to contemplate such actions. For the boys it was an opportunity and not to act on it was in every way contrary to the need they saw. In a way it was also part of the thrill that came from being on the edge of danger.

It was a similar thrill that gambling provided. There was the thrill of winning when the gamble paid off, but there was also the excitement that came from the consequences of losing. Nobody wanted to lose, but the fact that loss was part of the gamble made it irresistible. Everybody knew that getting too close to the flame you could get burned. The challenge was to get as close to the flame as possible without being singed. That was the real thrill!

With Michael the gambling started when he was around fifteen years old and getting more closely in contact with the neighborhood street culture. Like the rest of the way things went out on the street, gambling followed suit. It started with pitching pennies, then betting a nickel a card when playing Hearts. From there the bets and the 'games' gradually accelerated until it was a dollar and five dollars in the pot. When someone lost in one of these 'games' it could be a few hundred dollars and where was that money going to come from?

There were two ways to pay off a debt if personal funds were not an option. There were loan sharks willing to 'process' a loan that had astronomical interest rates with payoff terms starting the week after the loan was granted. If it wasn't possible to pay the principle plus the 'vig' it could go in two unpleasant directions; one, the loan would grow geometrically with the principle and previous 'vig' being juiced with another 'vig' ad infinitum until the debtor was so far in the hole there was no way out. At that point you were either beaten within an inch of your life or possibly beyond the inch to serve as an example to others who might consider not paying the debt. The other direction the payback could go was now you were 'owned' and could be called upon at any time to perform any activity that would advance the lender's needs. You would be held like a puppet on a wire performing actions directed by people who were known to do evil.

There was a second option for raising whatever money was needed. While dangerous, it was a hundred times better than dealing with the loan sharks. Yes, dealing with the cops and the law was a much safer, healthier way of obtaining the needed funds.

There were many easy targets in the neighborhood like the trucking company that warehoused many items and loaded them onto trucks to be delivered around the city and beyond. "We knew a guy from the neighborhood, Tommy T, who worked there".

Tommy was about ten years older than Michael and his friends and he had a responsible job at the company making sure the trucks got loaded properly and routed. So Tommy T had access to information that was important. The best trucks were the ones that were loaded with tools. Tools were the easiest thing to fence. People like mechanics and individuals who worked on their own cars were ideal customers. This was a working class neighborhood where the need for good tools at a bargain price made for easy sales. The most valuable of all the tools were the jackhammers used in breaking up concrete for new construction or in some cases for breaking through cement walls to get to valuables on the other side.

Of course, Tommy T was in this for his 'cut'. "He would tell us which trucks were loaded with tools, when they were scheduled to go out and where the keys could be found. It seemed like a great plan. We had an inside man with the Information we needed and we had the knowledge of where our customers were. One of the things that we didn't account for was that we were working in a very limited geographical environment; maybe a fifteen to twenty block area. How long would it be before someone caught on? How long after we crossed the line would we go over the edge?"

Yes, it was going to happen. It was just a matter of time. This was a rag tag operation that fell apart when a weak connection with a stolen cargo van was stopped by police. He was supposed to take delivery of the stolen goods on 38th Street and distribute them from there. When police caught him with the stolen van, this weak link believed if he 'spilled the beans' he would get off easier on the charge of stealing the van. He knew Michael and his four friends were part of the operation, but he was unaware of the role Tommy T played. As a result Michael and his friends were to be hauled into court to be tried for their crime, while Tommy T would never be implicated. Yes this rag tag gang would never turn on their friend. So as they prepared to meet the judge assigned to the case, Tommy T remained free and as a matter of fact spent several more years working for that trucking company.

First the boys had to spend a night in jail and the next day they were to be brought before the judge assigned to their case. Michael's friends acted and looked like clowns and wise guys when they came before the judge. Michael was smarter. He knew how to act in this situation and was keenly aware of what the consequences could be. When questions were directed to Michael his answers were respectful always answering yes and no questions with a humble, "Yes sir or No sir."

Michael was to be released in the custody of his father, but first the judge pulled Michael aside and escorted him into his chambers. The judge said, "I see something in you and I am going to give you a break."

The break involved Michael making a choice, "You can spend four years in a cell or you can volunteer for four years in the Marine Corps. You have two days to make a decision."

Michael noticed on the walls of the judge's chambers framed photos of the judge in his Marine fatigues as well as framed medals indicating the service he performed for his country.

Michael asked, "Are you a Marine?"

The answer was, "Yes, and now you have a choice to make."

Michael was shaken, but after his father picked him up they started talking like they never shared before. His father told Michael about his Navy service in World War II and the dangers he faced from the German U-Boats out to sink supply ships as well as any ships supplying reserve troops or involved in tactical operations. The night continued as they watched the movie 'The Sands of Iwo Jima' with John Wayne. It all seemed so strange that all these events were coming together. Was it a coincidence or a prompting by his father? Whatever it was, it left a deep impression in Michael's mind.

It was two days later, the day that Michael had to give the judge his decision, he was looking out the window of his apartment when he saw a Marine in dress uniform walking past the butcher shop about a half block from the Port Authority terminal. The way the man walked with such strength, authority and pride it became obvious to Michael that was something he wanted to be part of.

Before reporting to the judge, he headed down to the Marine recruitment center, which was not far from his home, near the Port Authority where he saw the proud Marine walking. He told his story to the Marine recruiter, including the criminal enterprise, being caught and the offer made to him by the judge; the Marine judge. The recruiter replied, "You're my kind of guy."

Michael signed up and headed over to the courthouse. He found the judge and they went to his chambers where Michael showed him the proof of his decision. The judge wished Michael good luck and told him that the only time he ever wanted to see him in this courthouse again would be when he was on leave and coming in to report his progress.

CHAPTER 4

OFF TO THE CORPS

Today was the day. One day after signing up to report for training. One day after seeing the judge that offered Michael a chance to change his life. Change indeed! His father, Menatti, had spoken to Michael about the Marines before he signed up saying along with a slap on the head, "Don't sign up with the Marines. They are the ones sent into dangerous situations before any other units are considered." Michael warned his father, "Don't ever hit me again, I'm not a child, I'm a man."

Michael was prepared to leave that morning, but his parents were nowhere to be seen.

"Didn't they remember he had just told them the night before that he would be joining the Marines the next morning? Didn't they know I was leaving? Was my father still smarting from my response after the slap on the head? Maybe my father pulled an extra late-night shift at the bar and was still asleep. After all it was 4:30 in the morning. But what about my mother, Angelina, she at least should have gotten up to see her son off. In any case the house seemed deserted. Maybe they just didn't believe I had actually joined the Marines and were not prepared to say goodbye."

After calling for them again and again he finally gave up, called a cab, picked up some loose change that was lying around and grabbed some of his father and mother's cigarettes.

Before he went outside to wait for his cab he left a note for his parents, "Sorry you didn't get up. Sorry I missed you. I will be joining the Corps and will be in touch."

He was lucky to get a cab since the taxi workers had just come off from a strike the day before. The cab pulled up and Michael gave the orders to take him to Fort Hamilton in Brooklyn. As they drove away, Michael asked the cabby to go around the block once more to see if anybody was looking out the window for him. There was nobody at the window.

Michael just said, "Go."

All of this added to the tenseness that under the best of situations was a traumatic transition in life for this eighteen year old.

Early in the morning, it didn't take long to get to Fort Hamilton in Brooklyn. As the cab slowly pulled up across the street from his destination, Michael could see the milkman making his early morning deliveries before the sun came up. He paid the cabby who seemed to sense the eeriness that Michael was experiencing.

All he could say was, "Good luck son." At that moment everything seemed so strange.

As Michael approached the building across the street all he could see was a huge barracks like building with imposing doors that opened into a huge gymnasium like setting. As he entered, the first group of enlistees he saw took up half the space within the building. These were the Army recruits. As he proceeded looking for the area where he was supposed to report, he next saw groups assigned to the Air Force and the Navy. Each of these took up a similar amount of space that appeared almost to consume the rest of the available space. Was he in the wrong place? Did he somehow miss the group he was assigned to? Then he saw them, a Marine Captain, a Sergeant and two recruits. They were waiting for two more recruits to be sworn in before leaving for Newark Airport. Those two never showed. Now was the time for the final commitment; the swearing in, the oath of allegiance to serve the country. Now they were ready to leave, but Michael was curious about the many other service members compared to this small group going into to the Marines. The Captain spoke in a proud and authoritative voice, "People are looking at us. You will walk taller and prouder than many. It only takes a few of us to do the job of the many you see here."

The pride that came from the Captain's few words, removed some of the strangeness that Michael was experiencing from the time he left his home early that morning. He thought, "This is pretty good. These guys are alright. I was injected with this special sense of pride. It made me feel at that moment of being part of something special. I was less uneasy and more comfortable."

The bus left for Newark Airport amid a raw, wet and miserable rain storm. When they arrived they picked up fifteen more new Marine recruits that had been sworn in. It was about 12:30 in the afternoon when a Corporal took roll call before boarding a small plane that could seat about ninety and before anybody realized it they were in the air headed for South Carolina. Up to this point, for the most part, Michael had not gone very far outside his neighborhood.

"We landed at the Savannah/Hilton head Airport and from there we boarded a military bus that would take us to Paris Island. It was only about a forty-five minute ride."

The bus driver, dressed in Marine fatigues, was very engaging and seemed like a really nice guy. He told those on the bus that if they wanted to smoke, they should do so know because once they reached the camp at Paris Island, there would be no smoking. It seemed as though there was this constant contrast between getting comfortable and being reminded about future discomfort. For the most part, everybody serving in the Marines up to this point seemed positive, inspiring and helpful.

As the bus approached the entrance to Paris Island, Michael would remember for the rest of his life what the large sign greeting those who entered read. It was a quote from the newsman and reporter Walter Winchell who had lost a son at war. It read, "If you have a son at Paris Island, pray for him, if you have a son in Viet Nam, write to him." Those ominous words would have their impact over time, words that would never be forgotten and whose impact could not be measured.

The eeriness began to creep back in. "All cigarettes went out as we entered the gates. The trees were dripping with Spanish moss, like it was something out of a bizarre horror movie. I had never seen anything like this in person."

They came to a barracks with a light on over a small door that opened to a larger door. Standing in that large door was one of the biggest men Michael had ever seen. It was the D.I., drill instructor, that would soon take charge of these young men. He came out of the doorway and stepped onto the bus.

"I couldn't believe it! The bus just rocked from side to side from the sheer size and weight of this man. I realized then that comfort and niceness was over."

As he entered the bus the D.I. began to bark out, "Alright you maggots, I want to see you marching asshole to belly button. Move, move, move! And you with the sunglasses, this ain't no beach." With that he knocked the sunglasses to the ground

The recruits were ushered into the next room. The D.I. commanded them, "Stand straight."

This was the 'Barber Shop.' There was no traditional barber's chair. There was no chair. Everybody's hair was shaved off. These men were not barbers, they were head shearers. From there they were transported into the next room.

"At this point we were given over to four men that would take charge of us for the equipment dispersal and eventually be our D.I. for the remainder of our boot camp". In this room they were sized up for the clothes they would be wearing for training. The D.I. began barking out his instructions, "Take off your clothes and put your name and address on them. They will be sent back to your home." This was the way Michael's parents would find out where he was.

Everybody was nude except for a jacket that would be part of their training clothes. Again one D.I., his voice dripping with contempt shouted, "Get in the shower! I don't want you carrying any of the dirt you brought here with you. But you still won't be fully clean until you get some Marine food in you and take your first shit."

Michael thought, "What did I get into. Whatever I got into, I think it's better than being in jail."

Into the next room was where the boots were distributed. They were warned to make sure the boots fit properly. The D.I. reminded them of their responsibility and their place in the scheme of things, "You are military property. Take care of your bodies." They would learn more about that.

Now the reluctant volunteers were fully dressed. It was late in the day and Michael hadn't eaten anything to speak of since leaving home that morning. One of the D.I.'s, at this point, they all looked the same, walked up and down the line of men straightening them out and making them stand tall.

"Now I am going to give you a treat. You are going to have duck for dinner."

Michael was starving since he hadn't eaten all day since leaving home early that morning. Any decent food would be great, but duck; that would be special. Johnson laughed sarcastically, "You are going to duck in and duck out".

Not only were they being rushed, but the food was what Michael would classify as 'shit on a shingle'. It was something resembling ground up meat and gravy on a piece of toast. As hungry as he was, Michael could not eat this particular type of 'duck'. The only food he could get down was some Jello gelatin and that was the extent of his 'duck' dinner. This first encounter with Staff Sergeant E.W. Johnson created a tension in Michael bordering on grievance

The main D.I. was relentless in harassing his future platoon. "When I'm finished eating my dinner, I expect that you will be waiting for me at your assigned barracks. I don't wait for anybody!" Everybody watched the D.I. to see when he would get up and then they would get up and hustle the approximately half mile to the barracks that were assigned, making sure that they arrived before Sergeant Johnson.

The barracks were buildings made with cinder blocks and concrete where every sound echoed and was intensified. The sanitary facilities while immaculate seemed insufficient for the number of men it needed to accommodate. This was the beginning of eight weeks of rigorous boot camp training. Normally boot camp was thirteen weeks, but the Viet Nam War was at a critical point and men were needed there, so the shortened boot camp would be extremely intense. Everything seemed to be rushed with little time and little space.

The rush and the perceived insufficiencies came fully alive the next morning. It started 4:30 in the morning with garbage cans banging around outside and the D.I. shouting orders. This certainly was not the corporate world where one would expect an orientation period. The noise and confusion was disorienting. "I'm not your mother, Johnson shouted, "You have five minutes to get yourself ready."

Five minutes for twenty to thirty guys to shave, shower and use the latrine. It just wasn't possible to do all that in five minutes. There was no time to think. Everybody was scrambling to break through the confusion. As they learned, that was the idea. They were being trained from the start to react to situations and not contemplate how they were to accomplish what seemed to be impossible. Without knowing it, they were learning how to work efficiently with others to accomplish a goal. What seemed impossible would eventually become routine.

If life teaches anything it is that nothing is perfect. There is always the chance that nature or individual personalities sometimes bend in ways that no matter the training, human vulnerabilities can alter outcomes. It was about the seventh week of boot camp, about a week before graduation, when a set of human vulnerabilities had their way. It was time to muster at 4:30 in the morning.

These young men had become an efficient and well-disciplined platoon, but something must have happened the night before that got under the skin of Staff Sergeant Johnson. It could have been something personal or perhaps some break in what Johnson perceived as to how things were typically carried out by those he commanded. He strode up and down the barracks that morning accompanied by Sergeant Perdue and Sergeant Pierce. Normally he was accompanied by a third man, Sergeant Ddrvane, but on this day Ddrvane was not present. Why he wasn't present was not known, but the fact he wasn't there would prove to be a stroke of good fortune for Michael.

Johnson, accompanied by his two aids, stopped in front of various men who were standing at attention in front of their bunks and he commenced shouting at them, regarding real or perceived violations. He then came to Michael's station. Michael was confused about what it was that Johnson was so upset about, but he knew that after he vented it would blow over. Not quite this time. Johnson started bellowing and shouting in Michael's face, but the worst was that he was nose to nose with Michael. Johnson was so close that as he shouted his bad breath and spittle that came with the anger landed in Michael's face and the odor entered his nostrils. This to Michael, without ever thinking, was a violation of his personal space. He reacted by throwing up his arms in an effort to move Johnson away from him. With that Michael's left arm hit Johnson's shoulder and his right arm brushed Johnson's face. In an instant both Pierce and Perdue pounced on Michael with one blow landing on Michael's right eye. The scuffle was over quickly and to Michael's good fortune the third aid, Sergeant Ddrvane wasn't there that day to add to the injuries.

Staff Sergeant Johnson along with Pierce and Perdue made their point and nothing more was said about the incident at this time, but Michael would meet Johnson one more time in the future, but not now at this boot camp. There was one more week to go for graduation. Michael was looking forward to seeing his parents and hoping his black eye would be healed by then.

It was graduation day. These men were the cream of the crop. Not everybody made it this far. Some washed out and others had to go back for retraining. But this group was a highly disciplined unit that operated as one well-oiled machine. To add to the drama and the specialness of the day, the fatigues normally worn throughout boot camp were sent to the cleaning trucks to be cleaned, pressed and starched. Each man made sure his boots were spit shined so they reflected like a mirror. The starched pants were then bloused at the top of the boots. The starched shirts with three creases in the back were then buttoned up the front with the top button left open revealing a crisp white undershirt. Michael would say, "It must be how the President of the United States must feel on inauguration day."

Parents were waiting in the bleachers to see their sons who had left as boys, but were now men in the true Marine sense. The sun rose behind the bleachers as the various platoons came out to pass in parade view. As they approached the bleachers the command went out, "Leeeft face."

With that, every foot lifted simultaneously as they pivoted on their left foot. It was a crisp turn as every foot hit the ground at the same time, 'Whoomp!' The sound could be heard across the parade ground.

The second command went up, "Eyes right!" All heads snapped to the right in tribute to the parents in the bleachers. It was as if their bodies were connected. They passed the bleachers in review and the awed parents couldn't believe what they were seeing.

When the ceremony was completed, each man had two hours to meet with his parents. Michael strode up the steps in the bleachers and came not more than four feet away from his mother, but she didn't recognize him; his hair cut close to his head, his body slim and hard as a rock. He had to remind her, "It's me, Michael your son."

She would reply, "Oh my god, you look so different; so skinny. Look at your eye. What happened? What kind of food did they feed you here?"

Michael reassured her, "I'm healthy, healthier than ever."

His father just looked at Michael with awe saying, "You don't know how proud of you I am. It is hard to find the words."

They spent the allotted time together, talking about Michael's training and what he would be doing next. Next would be Marine Corps Base Camp Lejeune in Jacksonville, North Carolina.

CHAPTER 5

CAMP LEJEUNE

Camp Lejeune, if you've never visited or had service that brought you there, is impressive in its location, structure and purpose. Yes, there is a reason Camp Lejeune is located in this coastal area of North Carolina. There are fourteen miles of beaches where amphibious assault training takes place and is located between two deep water ports that allow for the quick deployment of both troops and equipment.

It would not be long before Michael became part of one of those deployments. But before that would happen, the Marine Corps would experience the Hell's Kitchen remaining in Michael and would always be a part of his makeup, part of what made him a Marine who would serve his country in a distinguished manner. The path wouldn't always be pretty, but would always be with a final sense of duty.

When Michael entered boot camp at Parris Island he, like all new recruits, was tested to see what kind of special functions they seemed most adapted to. As it turned out Michael's aptitude leaned in the direction of food service. It was a call to serve in the mess hall. As in any job, one starts out at the bottom. The bottom in the mess hall meant peeling potatoes and preparing other vegetables for the line cook to use.

It wasn't long before Michael became one of the line cooks whose duties included getting to the mess hall at 4:00 AM to prepare breakfast for the men going out on various maneuvers and training. He rose to this position because he learned to be efficient with an orderliness that would keep the line moving so that breakfast could be served in a prompt, competent fashion. In this way the Marines going out for the morning could get to their assignments without having to cram food down in order to get their job done.

Gunnery Sergeant Rickles who was in charge of mess hall operations, noticed that Michael had abilities beyond cooking. He noticed the organizational skills along with the ability to motivate others to complete a task. So he was sent to work in one of the offices that processed paper work for many of the military decisions including such things as granting leave, length of leaves, transportation, processing change in rank and the accompanying pay that the Marines would receive. He would learn the business of the office and how the organization worked. Maybe he did not have a formal education, but he was smart and along with a friendly personality and Hell's Kitchen street smarts, opportunities began to arise.

This assignment was always meant to be only part of Michael's responsibility which actually worked to his advantage. The kitchen remained critical to Michael's growing influence and ability to bend the system to work for him. Part of his kitchen duties was to order the ingredients needed to make the baked goods. As a result, this lead to a relationship with a Marine baker who came from the Hampton's on Long Island. This baker had connections from his previous work before entering the service. These connections included people in the liquor industry. The baker knew that sugar was a valuable ingredient in the making of alcohol, so he let Michael know if he could supply the baker with additional baked goods that Michael produced then he might be able to get additional quantities of sugar for Michael. What part of the industry he was involved in was not known nor was it asked. Transactions always were tit for tat; the more you gave, the more you got.

Connections weren't just connections for social purposes. Yes, social connections were important for developing relationships that were mutually satisfying, but along with that social element came a system where each person's talents and abilities led to an organization that could achieve concrete goals.

Michael had to have his work and dress clothes cleaned on a regular basis. The cleaning truck would come around at a predetermined time each week and Michael would have his laundry picked up. With his outgoing, curious and inventive personality, he would strike up conversations with the cleaner. It came out that Michael could get extra sugar from his Long Island contact.

The cleaner asked, "Can you get me some?"

"Sure I can!"

The first delivery Michael made was a couple of pounds of sugar. When he brought them to the cleaner the cleaner exclaimed, "That's it! I need hundreds of pounds because my Southern friends are making liquor."

Michael would have to use his connections in the motor pool to deliver that much sugar.

There weren't enough baked goods to trade for that much sugar so Michael gave his Long Island baker some of the liquor in order to get more sugar. Good old American entrepreneurship, converting an excess into a profit. Booze was a very valuable, tradable commodity.

The cleaner's brother was a pilot for Piedmont airlines so the pilot wanted to show his appreciation for what Michael was doing to help his brother. What better way for the pilot to express this appreciation than to offer Michael free airline passes whenever he took leave. Another tool in Michael's expanding tool box.

Michael's talents began to extend into his office work. He was doing such a great job he was promoted to Private First Class. He was very aware of the raise in pay coming with a promotion and became curious what future promotions could mean. With such curiosity, personality, organizational skills and Hell's Kitchen street smarts, the possibilities seemed unlimited. Soon Michael would be promoted to Lance Corporal as he was recognized for his ability to get things done while maintaining discipline among those he was in charge of. Those above rank to Michael saw that he got the job done and they didn't bother to ask how the job got done. There certainly was no place for outright disregard for the rules and regulations, but if one knew how to work with and around those rules and get the job done, there was no problem. Michael was an expert.

Gunnery Sergeant Rickles saw much about Michael that he liked, so much so that he gave Michael extended leaves anywhere from twenty-four hours to ninety-six hours. Michael understood and appreciated what Rickles was doing for him and made sure not to abuse these privileges, but on the other hand saw the usefulness of rewarding others by transferring his leave privilege to them. Not exactly within the rules, but what was the harm when the results lead to a well-organized and disciplined control of the barracks which had become among Michael's responsibilities.

In the barracks, the sergeants slept in separate quarters. They would muster the men and check them out before heading to the day's assignment. Michael as a lance corporal in those barracks made sure the men were ready when the sergeants came to call. The sergeants appreciated the order and the men liked the idea of being in a position where they were not going to be hassled. Michael used his power to give and take much like the bull fighter who knows when the bull needs encouragement and when the bull needs to be brought under control. Michael had the tools and knew how to use them.

Gunnery Sergeant Rickles appreciation for Michael came to a point where Michael was treated like part of his family. Michael would be invited to dinner or a barbeque where Rickles' wife would be part of the family environment

Rickles' concern for Michael's future became apparent when he suggested that Michael should consider getting a GED. He felt this would improve Michael's chances for future promotions. This high school equivalency diploma along with Michael's personality and leadership skills could lead to a career in the Marines or if he decided to enter the business world after the Marines it would make him a very attractive candidate

While Michael was appreciative of what Rickles suggested and took this advice to heart, he was not ready or willing to do the kind of studying it would take for someone who left school when he was thirteen and at that was never much of a student.

But the wheels never stopped turning. There was always a way to get around the roadblocks. All that was needed was the right set of circumstances.

Michael had his connections in the mess hall and he had his connections in the office and of course his relationship with Master Sergeant Rickles made for a trifecta any betting man would find attractive. Finding the right horses to run and the perfect conditions would make it an even better bet. Gambles are never sure, but some are just better than others.

Lieutenant Rittenaur ran the office where Michael would fill in when he wasn't running the mess hall. Rittenaur observed over time that Michael knew the intricacies of how the office worked and in addition had great rapport with the rest of the staff. In Rittenaur's mind, Michael would be able to keep the office running smoothly if the Lieutenant had to or wanted to leave for a short time.

Private First Class Cosby was a young college graduate who because of his educational background was an ideal candidate to do the office work required under Lieutenant Ritenour's command. In age, Cosby was Michael's contemporary which led to conversations young men would have and in one case the conversation turned to Michael's lack of a high school diploma. Michael expressed his concern about taking the GED test. Cosby laughed it off saying, "Oh, you'll fly through it. You shouldn't have a problem."

Finally all the horses lined up. Rittenaur needed to leave for several days, so he went to Gunnery Sergeant Rickles and asked if he could release Michael from his mess hall duties in order to run the office in his absence. Rickles agreed immediately with a sense of pride that his protégé would be trusted with such an assignment.

When Rittenaur left, Michael was the highest ranked person in the office. Michael was a lance corporal and Cosby was a PFC. The only other person was a civilian woman. Michael was in command. The first thing he did was to pull Cosby aside and asked, "How would like a ninety-six hour pass, two weeks in a row?"

Cosby responded, "What? What do you mean? How can you do something like that?"

Michael said, "I have a plan for you to take the GED test for me. You said I could fly through it. You are going to be me for a week."

Michael began to lay out the plan. The plan was somewhat sketchy and seemed to need a little bit of luck for it all to work. There would be four days of tests and each day PFC Cosby had to be able to show that he was in fact Lance Corporal Secli. Right from the first day it all could have fallen apart except for some luck and fast thinking and talking by Michael.

When Cosby got to the test site the first day, all he had was Michael's name tag. He didn't have the registration card and wasn't wearing the lance corporal stripes. The captain at the table was a little perturbed and asked, "What's going on here? You are not prepared Lance Corporal? Go inside and I will have to call your office."

When the Captain called the office, Michael picked up the phone. The Captain asked, "Who am I speaking to?"

Michal answered, "PFC Cosby."

The Captain continued, "Is Lieutenant Rittenaur there? I have Lance Corporal Secli here to take a test and he does not have his paperwork!"

Michael answered as PFC Cosby, "No sir Lieutenant Rittenaur is out right now, but I'm in charge while he's gone and we will make sure he has all the proper paperwork when he comes back tomorrow. Please let him go ahead with the test."

"OK Cosby", said the Captain, Make sure this doesn't happen again."

There always needs to be a little luck in every horse race.

On Tuesday, the second day of testing, Cosby returned with all the proper documentation. It was the same Captain at the door and this time Cosby said, "Sorry about the problems yesterday sir. Thanks for your understanding. Everything is in order today."

The Captain shook his head with a little smile saying, "Just get in there and do your best."

On the third day there was a new person in charge of the testing site who was a lieutenant. At first Cosby was a little taken aback thinking that this was a new set of challenges getting past an unfamiliar person. But there were no further problems since he was fully registered as Michael Secli.

When Cosby came back from testing that day, Michael told him that no matter what happened he would be giving Cosby a ninety-six hour pass after the final day of testing on Thursday. Michael, as always, was good to his word and covered for Cosby through his ninety-six hour pass until that next Monday. On Monday Cosby was back and they both went back to being who they really were.

It seemed like everything played out really well for Michael and now all he had to do was wait for the test results to come back. That same day he got a call from Major McMahon who was the person in charge of base operations. The first thing that went through Michael's mind was, "The plan has been discovered and now what were the consequences going to be?"

Up to the Major's office he went with this sick feeling in his stomach. Not only would he get in deep trouble for this game, but Cosby would get jammed up as well. He entered McMahon's office, "Lance Corporal Secli reporting sir."

"Have a seat Lance Corporal. You did very well on your GED test. Congratulations. I'm happy to see that you are taking advantage of the programs that we offer on the base."

Michael left the office, wiping a little bead of sweat from his brow. The gamble had paid off and the horse crossed the finished line with impressive grades.

All of these contacts became part of Michael's universe. From the leadership at Camp Lejeune to the young Marines he shaped up in the barracks, Michael was seen as a person you could count on to get the job done. Through it all he respected those who were his commanders and those of whom he was given to command. It was coming close to the time to leave Lejeune and these friends and take the next step in the journey that would bring him to Viet Nam.

CHAPTER 6

THE LINE BETWEEN IS THIN[1]

Michael fought to survive from the day he was born in the bowels of Hell's Kitchen to the day he was forced to leave and join the Marines. It was not the gentrified Hell's Kitchen of the twenty-first century, but the Hell's Kitchen of the 1950's and early 60's where one fought for everything they had or figured out a way to get it. The expression, 'By hook or by crook', would be an accurate description.

The skills he developed and the mistakes he made working through the challenges and deprivations became integral elements influencing his survival skills as well as elevating his standing among those with whom he worked.

To say it was all good would be a lie. Deprivation and struggle are not generally considered to be inspiring. Overcoming deprivation and struggle is where the inspiration arises. Overcoming these elements by cheating, stealing and lying is not the glorious story book way in which a person should respond and grow. There is great sympathy and compassion for those who go without food and are starving, but when those same people steal food they are likely to be seen as criminals.

What are the boundaries? We have to have boundaries or we would live in a world of continuous chaos. Maybe it comes down to paying a price for stepping on the other side of the line or maybe it's the reason why one steps across the line. Then again perhaps it is the good or evil that is created when that line is crossed. In any case it appears that the line keeps moving or gets thinner at times.

As Michael continued his journey to Viet Nam, he brought with him all the survival skills he had accumulated over his short life; the strength and will to fight, the cunning to get what was needed and the leadership to get others to work with him to accomplish a goal. All this and more would be necessary to face the hell that was to come.

CHAPTER 7

ROAD TO DANGER

There would be three more stops before hitting the deadly beaches of Viet Nam. Each of the steps was one more level of escalation preparing for that day and the days to follow.

The first stop was Camp Pendleton on the outskirts of Los Angeles. Michael's plane landed in LAX, the international airport in Los Angeles. This was all totally new territory for a young man who was actually still a teenager. Just nineteen years old, his totality of experience involved Hell's Kitchen and military bases with very little experience outside that existence. Yes, he made his mark in those places, but they were limited environments. It was just another challenge for Michael.

The early May air was balmy and Michael dressed in his summer fatigues looked every part the Marine he had become. Secure with his place, he hailed the first taxi he could get, exhibiting that demeanor that came with being a Marine.

Before he left for Pendleton, his father encouraged him to see an old friend from the neighborhood who now owned a small hotel, more like a bed and breakfast, not that far from the airport. Since he had a couple of days before reporting to camp he made arrangements to visit the friend. Michael gave the cabby the address and off they went.

As the cab pulled up to the address there was only one problem, a big problem! The bed and breakfast was on the other side of the highway and apparently the cabby must have had another fare waiting or perhaps he had another reason unknown to Michael, because he wouldn't take Michael to the other side of the highway. Apparently to get to the other side of the highway meant perhaps at least a mile before being able to exit and turn around.

The highways, or as they called them freeways, in the LA area were huge six and eight lanes across with fences and massive concrete center dividers. There was no way to cross on foot. Michael could see a light up ahead and thought maybe there was a way to cross there. Still there was no way to cross. Michel stood there trying to figure out how he could get across to his destination, getting more and more frustrated by the minute. As he pondered his situation a car pulled up and when the window rolled down Michael saw an attractive young woman.

She asked, "Hi Marine. Where are you going?"

Michael was a little stunned exclaiming in his Hell's Kitchen skepticism, "Why are you a cab driver?"

"Oh no, I'm not a cab driver. You just looked like you could use a ride."

As she got out of the car to speak to Michael, he could see that she walked with a limp. He found out later that she was in a serious auto accident that damaged her leg. It was an injury doctors were never able to correct. But she was beautiful with short black hair, an attractive round face with alabaster skin that seemed to be lit from within. All of this was framed with a simple but elegant pair of golden hanging earrings. Her clothes were plain yet attractive. She looked like a girl you would bring home to mom.

"So what's your name Marine?"

Michael was still a little shocked and bewildered, but managed to stammer and get his name out. They then both got back into the car and she drove to the next exit where they could turn around and get to the other side of the highway. As they pulled up to the small hotel Michael thanked her for the ride, still didn't know her name, hadn't asked and said, "Maybe I will run into you again someday."

"It would be possible if you took my phone number."

Michael being a little flustered said, "Oh, thank you."

She gave Michael her phone number and since Michael never asked she told him her name was Jacqueline.

Michael recovered enough to say, "I will call you as soon as I get settled in."

Michael got out of the car and Jacqueline waited for him to enter before leaving. As he entered the little hotel he saw a women waiting behind the registration desk. As he approached still a little disoriented from his experience with Jacqueline, "I'm looking for Frank Raimondi."

The woman replied, "Who should I say is asking?"

"Michael Secli."

"Oh Michael, I can't believe it. I'm Frank's wife, Rose. It's so nice to see you! What a nice surprise. My god, you look just like your father, Menatti. Frank will be so happy to see you. He's not here right now, but he will be back soon. You look hungry. Stay. Have something to eat."

Michael could smell the sauce cooking in the back and yes he was hungry.

"Come on, she said, we have rigatoni, meatballs, spare rib, eggplant Parmigiana. Would you like some veal cutlets?"

"Wow, Michael thought, this is the great Italian Sunday dinner that celebrates family."

The veal cutlets would not be necessary to add to what Michael saw as a feast.

"No, no, this is plenty. Thank you."

"Please stay with us before you have to report to your base." Let me take you up to your room so you can get settled."

This was a great opportunity for Michael because he had two days before he needed to check in at Pendleton. He didn't want to spend two days on base when he could stay in this comfortable family environment with old friends.

At dinner, Michael met Frank Raimondi and before they sat down they insisted that Michael call his mother and father. He told his parents how pleased he was to have a nice room, great food and such good people.

As they sat down to dinner Michael talked about his experience getting there and the amazing girl he met.

"Wow you're a fast worker," Frank exclaimed.

"It wasn't anything I did. It just sort of happened."

"Well, give her a call!"

"I will."

So, after dinner Michael called Jacqueline. He told her where he was going to be staying at the hotel where she dropped him off. He was a little uncomfortable as he tried to set up a date.

"I know it is 6:30 and maybe a little late, but if you would like to go out for coffee or a drink. (At that time eighteen was the drinking age in New York) I don't know what you do here in California."

"How about tomorrow", countered Jacqueline. "I'll pick you up, I'll show you some sites and we can spend the day together."

She picked Michael up that next day at around 10:30 in the morning. They spent the day together and Michael got to see places he never would have if it weren't for this relationship that had developed in a most unusual way; a taxi cab driver that maybe had an axe to grind and young girl who saw a man in uniform who looked like he needed some help.

Jackie wanted to know more about Michael. How long would he stay here? Where would he go after camp Pendleton?

"My prom is coming up soon and when I graduate I want to go to school to become a nurse. My father is going to have a little party for me tomorrow night and I would like you to be my guest. I know you have a few days off and I would like for you to be there."

As Michael tried to absorb all that was so suddenly happening and his only reply was an enthusiastic, "I would love to come!"

The next night Michael thought Jackie would come to pick him up, but to his surprise it was her brother who came to the hotel door. Michael would soon understand why as they approached the house which while not a mansion was very nice and the Anaheim community was filled with homes of some very financially well off families. Jackie's family was part of that environment and as he found out, her father was a very successful pharmaceutical sales executive.

Jackie's mother brought Michael in to the living room where they stood at the bottom of what looked to Michael like a long stairway coming down from what appeared to be the upstairs bed rooms. As he looked up the stairway he saw Jacqueline begin to descend with several of her girlfriends. She looked stunning in a lovely reddish pink gown and a magnificent pearl necklace draped around her neck descending into her bodice. She was a sight to behold, as with each step her gown would reveal glimpses of her legs. There was just enough to accent her beauty and yet obscure her injury.

Many of Jackie's girlfriends also brought dates and among those chaperoning their dates was one guy from the Army and another from the Navy. This was a family that evidently valued the military and those who gave service to their country.

It was a great party where Michael was made to feel very much at home. But like many roads in life, this was a side road and Michael was headed down a highway where the speed would continue to accelerate. He was headed back to base the next day, but there was still a prom to look forward to.

Training began that next day. This was a critical time in the training preparing these Marine's for the challenges they would face in Vietnam. Here they would learn to work with a team to accomplish a mission; the essential idea of working together to survive as a group responsible to and for each other. They would also learn how to use every weapon that a Marine on the ground needed to know how to operate as well as maintain. While the battles and encounters developed in training would come as close to real action as possible, nothing would ever compare to facing an enemy whose sole purpose was to eliminate you.

One of the initial exercises consisted of a team of six people. Normally, in combat a team consisted of four people, but for training purposes the team was larger to perhaps speed up the training. After all, soldiers were needed in Viet Nam as quickly as possible. They would get the proper training, but there would be some adjustments.

Each team was given a map and a compass, loaded into a covered transport truck in the dark of night, dropped off in a remote wooded area and then had to find their way back to camp. Along the route were posted guards with paint ball guns waiting to stop any team from reaching their goal and completing the mission. The only 'weapons' the various teams had where mock rifles similar to real weapons but offered no protection but rather served to remind these Marines that they were responsible for their equipment and had to carry them through the exercise as they would have to carry them in combat. This was no camping trip!

Michael was only nineteen years old, but he was a Lance Corporal, a noncommissioned officer, and despite the low rank he was obligated to take command if he outranked the others. Whether it was his rank or his natural instincts, he took command of the team.

His first action was to get the team together to lay out a plan to return to camp without losing anybody or leaving anybody behind. Michael, being Michael, had a creative plan that his team was fully into and committed to. It was not what the designer of the exercise had in mind, but rather it was the Secli way of getting results.

The team found themselves at the base of a hill. And Michael knew that if he was able to get to the top of the hill he would be able to see the lights of Los Angeles and with a compass could determine the direction the team needed to take to get back to camp. With that in mind, Michael sent two team members up the hill to find the directions. While the two went up the hill Michael and the others held their position at the base of the hill.

When the men returned, they had their position clearly defined and now they were able to use the maps to return to camp. Now all that was left was to evade the guards who had the paint ball guns. For Michael this was a game he knew how to play. Evading and slipping by the guards was almost laughable, but it was about to get worse.

But there was still a prom to look forward to and May 1967 was rapidly approaching. While the road to Viet Nam loomed later in September, this time with Jackie would be a pleasant rest stop along the way. Michael had no strong romantic feelings, but Jackie would need an escort to the prom and since Michael never had a prom experience this seemed like the ideal meeting of needs.

Michael spoke with Jacqueline's father to reassure him that he would make this a special occasion and would rent a Marine dress uniform to add to drama and specialness of the event. In return, Jackie's father offered the family car so that this could be a proper date without parental interference. Her father was under no illusions as to where such a relationship might go. After all, Michael was due to ship out for Viet Nam via Okinawa Japan that July and who could predict what such a future might entail. Her father was well aware of what could happen. It was not only death, but also the ways a brutal war can affect an individual. He had great respect for Michael, but did not want his naïve and impressionable daughter to live in a world of illusion.

In May they went to the prom and both had a wonderful time. Michael was his gregarious self and Jackie just enjoyed the atmosphere and being with Michael who created this atmosphere in her mind. Perhaps Jacqueline still held on to a young girl's romantic dreams, but it was never Michael's intention to further those images and ideas. He just knew how to have a good time. This was a pleasant stop before going back to the rigors of training that would prepare him for Viet Nam. That training would become more intense and focused. July was not that far away.

It was around the end of May and all the social diversions had come to an end. It was all business now; the business of learning how to survive in a hostile environment. These last few stages started on what was called the 'John Wayne' course.

It was called the 'John Wayne' course, because they had to carry their rifles at their hips, ready to fire at an instant. There was a simulated jungle course lined with trip wires and booby traps. While they made sure they were clear of those obstacles, there were potential enemies in the trees and behind heavy foliage on the ground. Danger was lurking around every corner and added to that was the potential for a noncombatant, sometimes a child, to suddenly appear seemingly out of nowhere. Was it the enemy ready to turn on you? How were you to know? They were instructed to avoid shooting noncombatants. Not always an easy task when the enemy didn't wear a uniform.

While working his way through the jungle course Michael hit some of those that popped out of hiding who happened to be noncombatants. After the drill he was pulled aside by the platoon sergeant and reprimanded for killing a noncombatant. This was the beginning of a confrontational relationship with this platoon sergeant.

Michael would say, "How the fuck am I supposed to know if it's a noncombatant when they suddenly appear with no warning?"

Later when all the trainees were together after the exercise, a lieutenant went over the responsibility regarding noncombatants. Michael posed the question to the lieutenant about how in an instant you had to make a life and death decision and if you made a wrong decision you could be dead.

He was not told he was wrong. The Lieutenant just said, "You will know what to do when you confront these issues in combat."

Michael thought, "I will deal with my conscience later. A dead man has no choices."

One exercise in particular brought confronting the reality of facing death on the battlefield. It involved evacuating wounded to a chopper while under heavy fire. In the area where the chopper would possibly come in were sections designated by green flags, yellow flags and red ones. Each flag group indicated the level of danger. As a chopper came into the red zone the area was filled with smoke, machine gun fire and mortar blasts. The chop, chop chatter of the blades and the wash of force created by the swirling blades added to the urgency.

Not only did they have to evacuate the wounded, but they also had to unload supplies for those remaining on the ground. As they backed up toward the chopper they were spraying protective fire at the hidden enemy. Once into the chopper, two men would take position at the side doors to protect the wounded and two men would go to the front to keep an eye out for the pilot and copilot. It was as close to real as they would get in training. While it was close to the real thing, nothing would be comparable to actual combat. But these training exercises built the instincts and muscle reactions that would be necessary when confronting the real danger of combat.

The time was quickly approaching when the real dangers would be faced. This training period, the final training period was the culmination of all that Michael had gone through from the time he entered basic training. He was as ready as he ever could be.

It was early in June, time to move the journey to its final destination. The plane would leave from Pendleton with Marines bound for Viet Nam. There were no direct flights to Viet Nam. The first stop was for refueling in Anchorage, Alaska. It was only about a three hour layover and as the plane refueled and got checked out Michael and his comrades had time to get some food and a few drinks. Michael, always the charmer, attracted a few female patrons with his playful chatter.

Michael would say, "There were only a couple of hours available so there wasn't much we could do."

It was just one more rest stop on the road.

Once refueled the plane was ready to continue the flight to Okinawa, Japan. If the journey was to end in the hell that was Viet Nam, then Okinawa was the gates to hell. Upon landing the departure doors opened and Michael's senses were assaulted first by a blast of stifling humid air so heavy it felt as though it needed to be pushed aside in order to move past it. Worse than the stifling heat was the fetid odor that was pushed along by the humid air. It was as if they had landed near an open septic field. This was the introduction to the oppressive heat that would be encountered in Viet Nam. Michael would spend about a month in Okinawa preparing for the voyage to Viet Nam.

This was not the Okinawa of the twenty-first century. This was Okinawa in 1967, still a territory of the United States and would remain so until 1972. As might be imagined just one more level of tension to be worked through; a product of the times. It was a historical link to the past and an imminent reminder of the present. It was here that Michael met Marine Corporal Craig W. Tourte who would become a combat buddy and lifelong friend. Craig had arrived earlier in April and had settled in there a couple of months before Michael arrived. Craig thought Michael was the coolest person he ever met.

"He was a street smart guy from Hell's Kitchen that drank Cutty Sark Scotch Whiskey, smoked unfiltered cigarettes and always looked 'squared away' with never a hair out of place."

This would be the base from which both Michael and Craig would soon land on the coast of Viet Nam for the first time. These Marines landing in Viet Nam would not be landing in planes.

CHAPTER 8

HITTING THE BEACH

It was early July, 1967, and time to leave what eventually would seem like the cozy confines of Okinawa. Michael along with his landing party, tanks, trucks and other cargo needed for their destination on the beaches of Dong Ha via a short stop in Da Nang, started loading on to the LST Washtenaw County 1166. LST stood for landing ship, tank. These were not the pretty sleek ships that sailed on the ocean. This craft was designed to land troops and equipment directly on to beach fronts. That meant it had a flat hull and wide doors in the bow for loading. When the doors closed they became a moderately pointy bow allowing it to be sea worthy.

Imagine being on the open sea with such a craft. Every wave would be felt as the LST heaved up and slapped back down. The bigger the wave was, the rougher the ride. Of course the bow was not as sleek as would be found on ships designed to sail on the ocean so the LST did not cut through waves as efficiently. So in addition to the heaving and slapping came the jolting as the bow smashed into waves. Not a ride that would be popular at amusement parks

There would be close to two hundred men on this LST along with all the equipment. One could only imagine what the 'living quarters' would be like. The smell of diesel from all the equipment along with the General Motors diesel engines powering the craft and the rough ride led to many sick Marines on the journey that would take about six days. They would travel about 1500 miles at speeds not more than twelve miles per hour before reaching the beaches of Da Nang and Dong Ha.

Michael's father, Menatti, had served in the Navy and knew enough about ships on rough seas; enough to recommend that it was best to choose a top bunk when settling in to the sleeping quarters. Rough seas create nausea and nausea often led to vomiting. The simple laws of gravity were indeed part of the bunk choice.

Leaving Okinawa put Washtenaw County 1166 into the Philippine Sea which actually is an extension of the North Pacific Ocean. If the ship was to travel east, the next land fall would be Hawaii. The LST would be on the open sea for about half the trip until they entered Taiwan. After sailing around the tip of Taiwan, they reached the South China Sea which seemed almost like a river to Michael. The water became much calmer, most likely because the South China Sea had Taiwan and the

Philippines as buffers between the North Pacific Ocean and the China Sea.

At night men would go out for a smoke and to exercise, but during the day they would meet in squads at different times for instruction. These squads would break down to ten or twelve men since there would not be enough room to handle more than that. Here they would go over tactics, clean equipment and generally get filled in on what to expect. Sometimes it would be Michael's Gunnery Sergeant leading the instruction and other times it might be a Lieutenant or a Captain.

Between the Philippine Sea and now the South China Sea the Washtenaw County 1166 was on the open water for about six to seven days. Some of the trucks and other supplies that were being carried had to travel to Da Nang where it was needed. While Dong Ha was where the Twenty- Sixth Marines would eventually disembark, they had to pass that point and then return after delivering the cargo destined for the base in Da Nang. This would add another two or three days to the trip.

As Craig Tourte recalled, "We unloaded some vehicles and supplies that were needed in Da Nang and took on some additional supplies that were needed to support us in Dong Ha and eventually Khe Sanh."

After one or two nights in Da Nang the Washtenaw County was stocked with its new cargo, it was time to get to the final destination for these men and supplies to leave this LST.

Michael remembers as they approached the mouth of the river, "It seemed as though we were entering a storm. At first it was what sounded like distant thunder. There was a faint 'boom' 'boom' which gradually got louder and louder. The sound was accompanied by flashes of light in the sky. It seemed like thunder and lightning."

For sure it was a storm they were entering, but this storm wasn't thunder and lightning. These were canon flashes and exploding shells hitting the beach where Washtenaw County 1166 would unload its men and equipment.

The closer they came to the beach the louder the booming became until the shells landed so close the sound became deafening and the flashes were blinding. Michael knew that his job was to get onto the beach and begin to work his way with the rest of his group to the base at Dong Ha. It was Michael's first attempt at a beach landing and as he waded into the surf mortar shells were hitting into the sand all around. It wasn't an explosion, but more a 'thud', 'thud' as the mortar shells hit the sand. Michael was just four steps into the sand.

"Shit was flying and people were dying".

Suddenly he was hit from behind with what amounted to a vicious tackle. If fans were watching a football game they could have heard the tackle in the stands.

"What the fuck", he thought looking around to see where that came from.

He was hit from behind by a Sea Bee who was helping to facilitate the landing, shouting, "Get down. Stay low".

It wasn't the only advice he had to give Michael. After the attack was over the Sea Bee helped Michael up, "Marine hook up with someone who has been here one hour before you. That will give you another hour that you will be alive You got to listen to these sounds coming in."

And like a ghost the man was gone. There were wounded all around, but like a driver who can't remember how he got from point A to point B, all Michael could remember was falling asleep on the beach and waking up (was it the next morning?) having the feeling he was in the movie Apocalypse Now. While he tried to account for the time after leaving the Sea Bee and getting up on the beach, it became apparent that his mind just shut down as a form of protection so he could focus on what was needed to protect himself and those around him.

Most of the men and equipment were transferred into another type of landing craft that was smaller and more capable of navigating the Cua Viet River on the trip up to Dong Ha. It was around July 31, that Craig Tourte recalled as the first time they entered a battle area in Viet Nam.

CHAPTER 9

ON TO KHE SANH

It was only about an hour and a half to travel to the base in Dong Ha and from there on to Khe Sanh. Dong Ha was just a stopping point where Michael and his fellow Marines would receive additional instructions on what to expect and how to prepare for what would be a combat zone. No matter the preparation it would never make the reality any easier. Michael would also meet his commanding officers who would be with him at Khe Sanh. They all would be in Dong Ha for only about half a day; just enough time for some brief instructions and evening chow before heading to the barracks to sleep.

The sleeping quarters, while referred to as barracks, were actually rudimentary structures consisting of screening or netting to protect against mosquitoes and aluminum sheeting that served as roofing. In these circumstances it was a welcome relief and a place to lay their heads down and get some much needed rest. Michael would find later that these 'barracks' would actually seem like heaven compared to the conditions he would soon face. The problems ahead would be more than mosquitoes.

All of those who traveled with Michael on the Washtenaw County were part of The Third Marine Division, but some would be going to other outposts where they were needed. Michael's unit, the Thirteenth Marines in support of the Twenty-sixth Marines would be heading to Khe Sanh after breakfast.

It was early August when they reached Khe Sanh. This location, this area, was new and beautiful to Michael's young eyes. What he saw was a beautiful landscape. He marveled at the lush valley stretching before him, leading up to the mountains rising in the horizon. Their camp would be the former site of an old French outpost just six miles from the Laotian border to the east and fourteen miles south of the DMZ (Demilitarized Zone). For the Marines its only use was the location affording a potential base for future operations cutting off the Ho Chi Minh Trail in Laos; a valuable supply line for the North Vietnamese transporting food, arms and ammunition to troops in the south all the way to Saigon.

War has a way of turning things inside out. The mountains that provided majestic beauty to Michael's young eyes would soon become fire breathing dragons belching out a smoky, deadly inferno raining down wrath on the Twenty-Sixth Marines. The beautiful, verdant valley would become a tangled jungle infested with enemy determined to finish the job.

However, there was little or no fighting when they arrived, but they knew that would change from the intel they were given when they left Dong Ha. So began the preparations for the fight to come. Each man along with a buddy began digging into the ground to create their own protective living space. Trenches, sandbags and whatever covering could be found to protect from the monsoons that would arrive formed this primitive dwelling. Individual ingenuity made for some interesting even elaborate structures. These structures were called a 'hooch'.

Michael would say, "Hooch is a home and home is where you dig it".

To this day Michael has a 'T' shirt with the words printed on the front, HOME IS WHERE YOU DIG IT.

Michael was a cook and an integral part in making sure the men were fed. This was no easy task. First there had to be a structure that would allow for food preparation and distribution. Since there were no structures built, they had to improvise by setting up a large tented area with a long table as a service area. Basically this was an open air facility that could afford no protection from shelling or other weaponry. There was little if any fresh food as those supplies were extremely difficult to get into such remote areas. It was basically boiling water and dried rations put together for a hot meal. Because of his organizational skills and the fact that he was the highest ranked individual as a Corporal in the mess unit, he was put in charge of the mess hall as it was and raised in rank to Sergeant.

As part of the mess team, Michael worked shifts like the rest of the crew. That meant he had 'time off' between shifts. Nobody really had time off under the conditions facing them. If somebody had a position like Michael's with 'time off' they would be responsible helping make repairs to the air strip, helping the Sea Bees dig trenches to store the ammo or driving trucks and other vehicles to get supplies from one place to another. Wherever help was needed that was where the shift workers went.

All through August and September it was almost as if the enemy was teasing them; a shell here and a shell there. This was when Michael's 'time off' was spent going out to gather information and protecting the doctor with whom he traveled. Captain Doc Lasker was a medical doctor who would travel into the Montagnard villages to attend to some of the medical problems of these native, quite primitive, indigenous people. While serving to help these native people it also served to initiate their help against the enemy.

The Montagnards were hated by the North Vietnamese as well as other ethnic Vietnamese, much like the hatred faced by many indigenous people no matter the country of origin. They were considered savages, given the derogatory name, 'moi'. They were befriended by the Americans and were willing to assist in any way they could; either by pointing out enemy locations and movements or actively engaging the enemy. The result would often end in gruesome deaths for the men of these villages.

As Michael walked through the village he noticed only women, children and some old men. The young men were either helping American forces or dead because they were helping Americans. These sorties with Captain Doc Lasker lasted only a couple of months when the Montagnard areas were overrun by the Viet Cong. They took the villages and used them to advance on the Twenty-Sixth Marines.

It was now October and the fighting for hills 861 and 881 was intensifying. These two hills were essential to control of the valley. When Michael wasn't working his shift in the kitchen he often was aiding the stretcher bearers taking the wounded and dead down from the hills. It was gruesome work that required an almost zombie like approach. If anyone let themselves become emotionally involved it could become paralyzing. This was the time where their training helped them to kick into an automatic mode. 'Leave no man behind', wasn't just a saying and if there wasn't enough of a man to bring back, they made sure his dog tags were retrieved. Joseph Conrad spoke of 'the horror' in his book, The Heart Of Darkness, and like the character Kurtz, each man faced the crumbling sanity around them and doing everything they could to push past the truth in front of them.

Eventually the shelling became more frequent. Rest, there was no rest. Any rest came when Michael came back to his hooch; that 'home' dug into the ground surrounded by sandbags, encircled by ditches to drain away the monsoon rains and covered by a flimsy roof composed of whatever materials that could be scrounged up. Yes, it was monsoon season and the rains kept coming, continually dripping through that makeshift roof. The men were constantly wet and at best damp. Just trying to keep socks and boots dry was a challenge. The conditions that could result from feet that were constantly wet, could lead to serious infections. It was another battle to be fought within the larger battle.

As the shelling increased, Michael just hoped that none of those rounds landed on his hooch. If that happened every man in there would be dead. Michael's hooch never got a direct hit. Others were not so fortunate.

Michael might say, "By the grace of God I was spared. I don't know why, but maybe it just wasn't for me to know."

It was approaching Christmas and the fighting was escalating. At this time no matter the training, the body and mind would become incapable of handling anything more. Michael, while not realizing it, was reaching that limit. Before the battle would reach a point where every man was needed, it was decided that Michael should get some rest and was sent for what was called R&R; the shortened form for rest and recovery.

CHAPTER 10

REST AND RECOVERY

The plan was for Michael to have a few days away from the combat zone. He left camp wearing the grimy torn battle fatigues he had worn for weeks since there was no rest or a clean change of clothes during the intense fighting. Michael was the last Marine you would expect to travel in such an unkempt manner, but this was a different time; everything was different. He was headed for Da Nang where he was to be flown to the peaceful beaches of Pa Nang.

Before he could get cleaned up and make his flight to Pa Nang, he was shocked to meet his drill instructor from boot camp. This was the same Sergeant Johnson with whom he had the physical confrontation that led to Michael receiving a black eye in addition to some scrapes and bruises. Michael never spoke with Johnson after that incident at boot camp and assumed that Johnson detested him and looked down at him as a troublemaking wise guy. Now he had to see this man again looking like some kind of derelict.

Michael stammered out an apology for the shabby way he looked, but that wasn't what Johnson was thinking. Little did Michael realize that the tough Sergeant Johnson respected him for his strength in standing up and not backing down. It all bubbled to the surface when they met. Looking at Michael in those tattered battle fatigues he said, "If I'm up in Khe Sanh when you are, I want to be in your fox hole."

With those few words, the respect of one Marine for another was conveyed in simplest and most sincere way.

By the time Michael got cleaned up and was issued some fresh clothes, he had missed his flight to Pa Nang. While he was disappointed, he just wanted to get his rest so he took the next available flight which turned out to be destined for Hong Kong. What did he know? He had never been to Pa Nang and never been to Hong Kong. Either would have been new to him.

New never seemed to deter Michael from adjusting to his surroundings. Reflecting back to that time, he thought of Hong Kong as comparable to Las Vegas. There was all kinds of action; music, glittery lights, bars and beautiful woman. Michael slipped into his Hell's Kitchen demeanor. With all this hustle and bustle he knew there those people somewhere nearby that would be ready to take advantage of what might seem to be an unsuspecting and naïve serviceman.

Michael hailed over one of the rickshaws that were transporting people around the city. He pulled the driver who was the owner to the side and pulled out a wad of cash saying, "if you watch out for me and avoid any problems while I'm here, this will be yours at the end of my trip."

Michael knew innately from the streets of New York that money talks when mixed with a smooth approach. It's kind of like good Scotch Whiskey; the expensive stuff generally goes down a lot smoother. With that in mind, Michael had a wonderful time and a much needed rest. This would be the last rest as he returned to the Khe Sanh base for what would be seventy-seven days of unrelenting enemy attack.

CHAPTER 11

SEVENTY-SEVEN DAYS

You Don't Know[1]

Do you know what it's like
To live in a muddy, stinking ditch
Clinging to life as all hell breaks loose
With staccato bursts ripping the ground
And acrid smells of gun powder
Permeating the air and filling your lungs?
No, you will never need to know.
Just hold me in your arms
And rock my soul like a baby
Until the sweating stops and ……..
I'm home again.
For Michael on Veterans Day 2019

On the night of January 21, one of the fiercest attacks, a part of the North Vietnamese Tet Offensive began, celebrating the start of the Lunar New Year.

The 'holiday celebration' commenced with a series of surprise and vicious attacks with everything the North and Viet Cong had at their disposal. It was fire and brimstone in the flesh, not just the rousing words of some gospel preacher.

Exhausted as a result of his continual duty under pressure from mid-February until this night, Michael's body and mind began to shut down. Going back to his hooch to rest, he fell into a deep sleep. He never heard a thing that horrible night, but when he awoke there was destruction all around.

"Holy shit, what the fuck happened here."

The airplane runway was virtually destroyed, planes were on fire and some hooches were gone as if they never existed. Casualties were high, but not only confined to those of the Twenty-Sixth Marines. There were Sea Bees, medics, truck drivers, support staff and photo journalists amongst those lost. All of them were trying to do what they were called to do regardless of who it was that called them.

It didn't take long to shake off the sleep and the shock. The base was under heavy attack with the enemy numbered somewhere between 20,000 and 25,000 strong. The trumpets were blaring and the enemy was charging their encampment.

"All of a sudden I felt like superman. It must have been the adrenalin that kicked in. Something went through my body and I felt like the sharpest and baddest ass walking the earth. I thought, what's, the worst they could do, kill me?"

Yes, adrenalin would account for much of that surge and the feeling of having superpowers, but Michael's training had taught him to fight. If not for that training then possibly the twin brother of fight, flight might have kicked in and retreat would have ensued. Michael wasn't alone; every man and the few women who were there, knew what they had to do as they confronted the charging enemy.

The Twenty-Sixth Marines and the Thirteenth Marines who supported them were highly outnumbered. The weather was horrible, making it virtually impossible to get air support. Without air support and the odds stacked against them it looked like defeat was inevitable. But for some reason the enemy did not take advantage of their superior numbers and overrun Michael's position. Perhaps it was the fierce defense and the losses inflicted on the enemy that made the North Vietnamese think there were more troops present than actually existed.

The idea of being outnumbered by an attacking force and turning defeat into victory or a stalemate has happened multiple times in history. While not the normal expectation, two famed examples are the battle of Marathon in 490BC and the Battle of Bull Run on July 21, 1861. At Marathon the Greek army should have been overwhelmed by the Persians who had far superior numbers. But the Greeks were able to lure the Persians into terrain that favored the Greek forces; open plains where the Persians were vulnerable on their flanks.

At the Battle of Bull Run, a small Confederate force was outnumbered by some 15,000 troops and defeated the ill prepared Union force that struggled in coordinating their units. The idea that they could run over the smaller Confederate units led to a confidence that softened their preparation.

These are just two of many examples where due to perhaps subtle reasons, a force with superior numbers was unable to convert that superiority into victory. History also tells us that victory in a single battle does not predict victory in a war. Despite the outcomes brave men and women fight to protect what they believe is right and just. Without that belief it merely becomes survival of the fittest. Then it becomes gladiators in an arena.

While the siege started on January 21, another heavy onslaught on the night of January 31, harkened the intensity that was to come. While the Viet Cong and North Vietnamese did not overrun the Marine emplacement, they were positioning themselves for further extreme and relentless attacks.

General Vo Nguyen Giap, the North Vietnamese defense Minister, was considered a brilliant tactician. Maybe his strategy was to soften the Americans with constant shelling and then overrun their position. Or perhaps his idea was to divert attention away from other areas of combat in the south that were more vulnerable. Whatever the strategy, the battle would rage on.

There was deep concern outside of Khe Sanh that the Marines would fall to the North Vietnamese. Comparisons were being made to the disastrous French defeat in 1954, at Dien Bien Phu. With that looming in President Johnson's mind, he ordered the military to hold Khe Sanh at all costs. From that first intense shelling on January 21, to the increased shelling on January 31, it was the job that Michael's Thirteenth Marines and those in the 26th Marines along with their support groups were called to do.

Colonel David Lownds was the 47-year-old commander of the 26th Marines. He was totally confident that his men could hold their position and inflict heavy casualties on the North Vietnamese. He presented a rather dashing figure with his British style military mustache.[2] While mustaches don't win wars, the confidence exuded by his leadership inspired those he commanded to fill themselves with that confidence.

Col. Lownds was sure the North Vietnamese would try to overrun Khe Sanh sooner or later. "It is only a matter of how much Giap is willing to lose. I would hope it would cost him 40,000 to 50,000 men, maybe more. What's there to panic about?' We're here to stay. That's our job. That's what we get paid for."[3]

Gunnery Sergeant Freddie J. Morris 36, from Thomaston Ga. said, "You can still see them out there, but not like we used to. They've had a hurt put on them some."[4]

Many in the Khe Sanh garrison almost welcomed an all-out enemy assault. PFC. Charles Hughes 20, from Chattanooga exhibited that bravado born of confidence. "I wish they would come in now. We'll kick them around a little, no question about it."[5]

The fact that finally they were able to get some air support when the skies started clearing was a big boost in the confidence level. Between the B-25 bombers and the jets strafing enemy positions and clearing away foliage helped prevent any further advancement. One had to keep in mind that the enemy was dug in trenches not more than 100 yards from the Marine encampment. Bombing had to be a precision endeavor. Khe Sanh was a landmark in the use of airpower in warfare_____ the first time that an aerial bombardment has denied an attacker the ability to assault his target.[6]

Michael would refer to those 100 yards as the 'killing field'. That stretch between the enemy and the Marines was dotted with Claymore personnel mines. For the enemy to risk attack, they would not only have to navigate the mined area, but also cross an area that had been totally defoliated by napalm leaving them open to being picked off if they decided to make an assault. The beauty that Michael saw when he first had arrived had now turned into a 'killing field' and the optimism and bravado by some Marines would soon prove to be the equivalent of 'whistling in the dark'.

While Michaels MOS (Military Occupational Specialty) was not combat arms, all Marines in time of war were infantry men. Michael was trained to be a cook and to efficiently serve the men assigned to him. But Michaels Gunnery Sergeant, Newman, who had served in both WWII and the Korean War was due to retire in six months. Those in command knew that the attacks on the base were about to get worse and that

Newman had done his duty with honor and decided not to subject him to what was to come. Newman was being sent home

A Lieutenant came over to Michael and said, "Secli until a replacement arrives for Newman, you are temporarily taking his position and will be in charge of these twenty-four men. Generally it's a staff sergeant who has at most ten men in his charge. Now Michael, nineteen years old, temporarily had twenty-four men that were his responsibility. It wasn't long that temporary became permanent. Now with these twenty-four men their duties were to guard the perimeter in the trench lines, build fortifications, man listening posts, assist with artillery suppressive fire and carry out the dead and wounded.

Michael, because of this new leadership position would have to send men into situations where they could be wounded or killed. While never trained to lead men, Michael had the instincts of a leader. When he saw the enemy, he stood up and started shooting. When his men saw him stand and shoot, they stood up and started shooting. It just grew from there. These men knew Michael would never ask them to do something he himself would not do.

"Were we scared? You're damned right we were scared. We were pissing in our pants. But when we got up and started shooting we got over that fear of dying right away. Leader, what leader? As soon as we were getting fired on I knew exactly what the fuck to do as if there was another choice".

Maybe it was that fluid, that simple, but perhaps there always existed this ability to lead people. Maybe it was in his genetics or maybe part of the many years on the hard scrabble streets of Hell's Kitchen where he depended on those around him and who depended on him to get whatever it was they were after. Whatever the cause, it translated into a man who was trusted by those in his charge to get them through this hell.

It's the words of Craig Tourte who served with Michael during the siege of the Khe Sanh base from January 21st to approximately April 9th, 1968 that gives a clearer picture who Michael Secli was and is.

"I am honored to have stood alongside you in the trench line, (in) a direct line of attack from the North Vietnamese Army. Together we fought gallantly, taking the brunt of the enemy's incoming artillery, mortar, rocket, sniper and small arms fire as some 20,000 North Vietnamese Soldiers, supported by tanks and artillery, swept down from the north toward the combat base.

Without your leadership, persistence, bravery and determination I am sure I, along with many of our comrades, would not have survived those horrific months. I recognize the decisions you made as our Sergeant were difficult and many were killed during that long and horrific action, but I am convinced (that) without your leadership many more would have perished".

There was an unexplainable, almost mysterious, dynamic or synergy that existed within Michael's unit that no doubt existed in other units like his. Each man's energy enhanced and increased the next man's energy until all that growing power made them a force with which to be reckoned.

"That's what made us such badasses."

As the days progressed they would need every bit of that energy they could pull from each other. The bunkers and defensive positions they lived in on the defensive perimeter reeked of foul and unforgettable body odor including urine and feces. There were no toilets or latrines to take care of those bodily needs. Sleep and rest were minimal and they were always exhausted. They were unable to wash or shower for months. Water, food and ammunition were constantly in short supply and had to be airdropped. Always they were cold and wet. Trying to keep feet and socks dry was a constant battle. Each man knew if their feet became infected, they were as good as dead. When boots and socks were put up to dry, it was then the rats nibbling on their toes and the spiders getting into the drying shoes.

On February 23, the peak of the North Vietnamese bombing came raining down. Using Russian made 152 mm cannons, their long tubes zeroed in on the besieged Marines when 1300 rounds slammed into the U.S. base. By night the North Vietnamese tunneled ever closer to the Marine perimeter.[7]

Yes, the Viet Cong and the North Vietnamese Army hit the Marines with every kind of artillery, mortars, and rockets in their arsenal. As the enemy seemed to creep closer still these men held their position. Because so many areas were under pressure that day, Michael had to let one of his men, Fred L. Thomas Jr., go to another location that was under heavy attack. Fred's position was overrun and Fred was killed. But still they held and the enemy was pushed back.

Back and forth the battle of Khe Sanh was unrelenting. It was now entering March, March 4, to be exact, when Michael sent Marine Donald B. Saunders on a detail to strengthen a defensive position. Saunders was killed when a mortar shell hit and exploded near him. It was the second man Michael had lost to this intense and dehumanizing battle. How many more would be lost and when would this end? The answers would never come without a 'but'.

It was close to three months wearing the same fatigues with which man wore from the start of the siege. By now they were soaked in blood and sweat and unmistakably filled with the odor of death. Some of the clothing was torn and some of it was rotting off their bodies. But still they held.

Approaching March 12, the battle at Khe Sanh seemed to be turning a corner. The monsoon was ending and more Air support came including the dreaded B-52 bombers. It now seemed that the 14th anniversary of Dien Bien Phu, would not end as it did when the French were routed and massacred. General Giap seemed to have come to the conclusion that he would not be able to repeat his earlier feat and stopped sending replacements to Khe Sanh.[8]

The North Vietnamese supply lines had been cut off by the intensive bombing to the point where the North Vietnamese troops existed on less than a half-pound of rice per day. Under most circumstances the enemy never would leave behind any of their equipment or supplies, but this time they left piles of valuable materiel. U.S. troops counted 182 rockets and mortars, 260,000 rounds of small arms ammunition, 13,000 rounds of larger caliber ammunition and 8700 hand grenades and mines. They had been badly whipped by U.S. airpower.[9] The fact remains that the 26th Marines with the 13th Marine reinforcements held that ground until the airpower could strike.

Not enough is known about this battle and the trauma these men went through. To understand to some small degree the strain of such combat, Swank and Marchand's World War II study determined that after sixty days of continuous combat 98% of all surviving soldiers will have become psychiatric casualties of one kind or another.[10]

Whether President Johnson knew this or not, he was deeply aware of the sacrifice these men made for their country. He paid special tribute for the heroism of those Marines who held that ground along with Sergeant Michael Secli and the Thirteenth Marines Reinforced who were all presented with a Presidential Unit Citation for their sacrifice.

Today Michael Secli's Marine service uniform as well as a photo of him in front of a bunker are exhibited at the National Museum of the Marine Corps in Triangle, Virginia near the Marine Base Quantico.

Presidential Unit Citation

PRESIDENTIAL UNIT CITATION to:
SGT Michael Secli, USMC, 2243483

**TWENTY-SIXTH MARINES (REINFORCED),
THIRD MARINE DIVISION (REINFORCED)**

for service as set forth in the following

CITATION:

For extraordinary heroism in action against North Vietnamese Army forces during the battle for Khe Sanh in the Republic of Vietnam from 20 January to 1 April 1968. Throughout this period, the 26th Marines (Reinforced) was assigned the mission of holding the vital Khe Sanh Combat Base and positions on Hills 881, 861A, 558, and 950, which dominated strategic enemy approach routed into Northern I Corps. The 26th Marines was opposed by numerically superior forces - two North Vietnamese Army Divisions strongly reinforced with artillery, tank, anti-aircraft artillery and rocket units. The enemy deployed to take advantage of short lines of communications, rugged mountainous terrain, jungle and adverse weather conditions, was determined to destroy the Khe Sanh Combat Base in conjunction with large scale offensive operations in the two northern provinces of the Republic of Vietnam. The 26th Marines, occupying a small but critical area, was daily subjected to hundreds of rounds of intensive artillery, mortar and rocket fire. In addition, fierce ground attacks were conducted by the enemy in an effort to penetrate the friendly positions. Despite overwhelming odds, the 26th Marines remained resolute and determined, maintaining the integrity of its positions and inflicting heavy losses on the enemy. When monsoon weather greatly reduced air support and compounded the problems of aerial re-supply, the men of the 26th Marines stood defiantly firm, sustained by their own professional esprit and high sense of duty. Through their indomitable will, staunch endurance, and resolute courage, the 26th Marines contributed substantially to the failure of the Viet Cong and North Vietnamese Army winter/spring offensive. The enemy forces were denied the military and psychological victory they so desperately sought. By their gallant fighting spirit and their countless individual acts of heroism, the men of the 26th Marines (Reinforced) established a record of illustrious courage and determination in keeping with the highest traditions of the Marine Corps and the United States Naval Service.

CHAPTER 12

IT AIN'T OVER

"It ain't over till it's over" Yogi Berra 1973

Like many of Yogi's famous Yogi-isms there is a deeper existential meaning depending upon the circumstances, an individual's experience and how each person deals with each experience.

In Michael Secli's case, the horrors of Khe Sanh are never far from his conscious mind and forever reside in his unconscious mind. It is something he lives with every day. There is the guilt over the death and injuries inflicted on the Marines to whom he was responsible. It was his duty to send them on perilous missions in order to protect their position and to find where the enemy was and when they might attack. When they didn't come back or came back horribly wounded, it was personal. To be directly involved with another individual's death or disfigurement was and is deeply personal. It is done, can't be undone and doesn't go away.

For two years after returning from Viet Nam, Michael would shower every day and sometimes twice a day trying to remove the red clay of the battlefield from is body. The clay wasn't there anymore, but to Michael it was still clinging to his body. If a car backfired or there was a loud disturbance, flashes of incoming mortars and artillery rounds lived in his mind. During the night, on many occasions he would walk the floor of the bedroom. His wife Lora called it 'night patrol'. There was no enemy present, but still they kept him awake. These events didn't happen every day but wouldn't go away completely for very long.

For Michael, deep personal feelings got locked away for many years. It was too real, too deep a wound to let out from the safety from where it was securely locked away. There were horrible atrocities he saw committed by the Viet Cong on mutilated bodies he came across while on reconnaissance missions. It was a kind of torture terrorism to demonstrate the power the enemy had to show what could happen if your ideas stood in the way of their ideology. Once an atrocity is committed, the next one becomes easier to commit until every action or response seems normal. Then the trap door opens, and morality plunges through into a dark abyss.

Michael would say, 'How can one human being be so cruel to another human being. You gotta be a sick mother fucker to cut someone's toes off, chop off their dick, stick a bayonet up their ass and rip their insides up their back, then poke their eyes out and stick sharp objects through their ears. How do people do this to one another. You can't understand how this is possible unless you were there. Why should I explain this? How could I explain this? So, I just kept it to myself."

Most of this Michael kept locked up for fifty years unable to express so many of the deep horrors of this war. But there were many other things the war left him with that would thrust their ugly head through that thin protective wall.

Michael dealt with these events by stoically proclaiming to himself or those who needed to know he was okay, "This too shall pass."

Viet Nam was like a junk yard dog. If the dog was chained up and behind the wall, it could do no harm.

Michael would be the first to say, "I wasn't a very nice person when I returned from Viet Nam".

While still in the Marines but now a Sergeant back in the states, he continued with and expanded his schemes using his position for personal gain and satisfaction. He used everybody from the motor pool to the cooks, to the cleaner and the cleaner's brother who could provide air travel for Michael if Michael provided him with enough sugar to make bootleg alcohol. He was skillful and adept at getting the job done, but there was an emptiness inside that needed to be filled. Fill it he did, but with a dangerous and destructive part of himself.

It didn't stop there. When Michael came home on leave, he reconnected with old family friends going back to the days in Hell's Kitchen and the Children's Aid Society. Joann was a friend from the time they were both five years old and were pronounced King and Queen of the Children's Aid Society summer festival. But that was a long time ago and now Joann was married to one of the wise guys that still held court in the neighborhood. Joann got Michael together with her sister Rosemary and they began dating while Michael was still in the Marines.

Eventually they married after Michael had served his time in the Corps, but still the emptiness remained. Now Michael filled the emptiness with multiple affairs and after a short time they were divorced. "We never should have been married. We were too young and had no idea who we were. But none the less we and I were rewarded with a beautiful daughter, Ria, who to this day is a gift that came from that unfortunate union of two people not ready for a life together".

Michael remained a bachelor for at least twenty years and continued a lifestyle that involved woman after woman with no intention of settling down. The emptiness was so deep and so wide nothing and nobody could add a thimble full of sense to take away the darkness.

Then one day in 1975, while tending bar in a small New Jersey town, a friend came into the bar with a woman he wanted Michael to meet. She was beautiful. She had dark hair, a creamy white complexion and a body that completed the picture. Her name was Lora. She was different from the girls he was dating. There was a classiness about her that Michael was not prepared for.

But still he was not ready to change direction someone like Lora would require.

It was another ten years, 1985, when Michael contacted his old friend who had introduced him to Lora asking if Lora was still unmarried and if his friend could arrange for them to meet. The emptiness was shrinking, and it was time to let Lora in if she was available and open to seeing him.

Yes, she was still available, remarkable considering a woman of such beauty and elegance was not already spoken for. And yes, she would like to see Michael. Maybe it was curiosity or maybe it was the unexplainable 'bad boy' attraction. Whatever it was, they both seemed ready to try. They dated for six years before being married, March 30, 1991. With a little devilish smile Michael said, "When she brought her toothbrush and a clean change of underwear to my apartment, I knew my old life was over".

In 1994 their oldest son Garrett was born and five years later Cameron joined the family. Things were good. Michael had a good job selling restaurant supplies and Lora was able to stay home and raise the boys. Michael was always part of the parenting and together they were giving the children the love and discipline they craved, while Michael was able to provide financial security.

In 2008, 'The Great Recession' turned the economy upside down. Michael and his family were not spared. Michael was scrambling to make ends meet. He was working two and three jobs just to pay the bills. The tensions were building and unlocking a side of Michael that was like fighting a war. That meant 'all hands-on deck' and when Lora was unable to bring herself to change her role from stay-at-home mom to working mom, the tension became explosive.

Any marriage counselor or psychologist will say that each person in a marriage bears responsibility for a healthy relationship. So, who was to blame. Each had their failings and Michael had the added burden of the ghost of Khe Sanh. This was another battle to be fought.

In Shakespeare's Julius Caesar, Cassius says, "The fault dear Brutus is not in the stars, but in ourselves". Shakespeare understood the part of human relationships where each person controls their destiny. Unfortunately, they became victims of history and economy over which they had little control. Divorce would follow in 2016, but over time they would learn about a love based upon respect for who they were and could become.

Call it the stars, fate or just life's reckless ride, the part that often derails the journey. The hopeful and courageous put life back on another set of tracks.

It had been fifty years since the start of the siege of Khe Sanh in 1968. It is a date that Khe Sanh veterans use to mark this event since many arrived and left at different times. A reunion of those Marines who served during the siege was planned to take place in Washington DC. Craig Tourte, a friend and combat buddy from that time and now serving as the Board Secretary for the Khe Sanh Veterans Association wanted very much for Michael to attend.

Michael was extremely reluctant to go, thinking that he did not want to rehash war stories and open wounds that he had worked to heal in his own way. Craig was insistent and reminded Michael that Bobby Galliano and Tommy Horchler would be there, and it would probably be the last time they all could be together as by now all were in their early seventies. Michael was not one to be easily cajoled, but this was as close to a call to arms that could come at this stage of life. You can't refuse your buddies in arms.

Yes, Michael was reluctant and apprehensive as he boarded the train for Washington DC in 2018, fifty years since the siege of Khe Sanh had begun. Michael was tired when he arrived, but Craig insisted he come down to the reception area at the Nugget Hotel this October 26, 2018. When Michael got down to the reception area, there was Craig holding up a sign, 'WELCOME SERGEANT MICHAEL SECLI'.

Craig greeted him, "Sarge you haven't changed a bit".

From there the apprehension began to dissipate as the four sat down at the bar, Michael, Craig, Bobby and Tommy. Many things were shared between these men that only they could understand. As they shared, it was if a cloud began to lift in Michael's mind. No therapy could have done more for Michael then what occurred between these four men. What he shared with his buddies freed Michael to talk to other Marines that were at the event, most of whom did not serve during the siege. They wanted to know what it was like and how they could prepare themselves for similar situations. With his newfound freedom, Michael was able to let them know how different it is for each person. He assured them that when it was time for them to act, if they had trained well, they would know what to do when their moment came. In his heart, he hoped they would never have to endure the deprivation he experienced but knew each had to face their own demons.

When Michael returned home after two memorable days, his sons Garrett and Cameron met him at the train station. As he got off the train, the first person to see him was Garrett.

"Wow dad you look twenty years younger!".

Who could have predicted the healing that took place in those two short days? From then on Michael began to add things to his life that gave him joy. While he was always a family man, now he got more pleasure in that role. He bought the Cadillac he always wanted, worked on his golf and played more often, started dancing which he had never done before, became more socially active and in general appreciated and wanted to enjoy what he had.

From the beginning, Michael always had a way that attracted people. He was handsome, well-spoken and knew what to say and how to say it at the right time. It might have gotten buried to a degree during those long years after Khe Sanh, but it was always there and often surfaced. But now he was like a lighthouse showing the way and keeping watch. That same light was attractive to anyone who arrived within that beacon. It was obvious to the doctors, nurses, receptionists and technicians involved with his prostrate treatments. They would seem to light up when they saw him and greet him warmly.

It was a new life, a kind of resurrection. Then one day as part of his prostate treatment a certain chemotherapy protocol was injected into his testicles. It was part of a prescribed therapy, so he was sent home with instructions to have someone stay with him that evening. His sons Garrett and Cameron wanted to make sure their father was comfortable.

Michael fell asleep from exhaustion that evening, but it wasn't long before his sleep was broken with horrible flashbacks. The enemy was charging, and Michael was shouting orders and asking questions.

"Watch out! Move! Go, go, go! Incoming! Hit the deck! Watch those son-of- a -bitches on your flank! Where the fuck is Saunders!?" On and on it went for what seemed like forever to his two sons while it only lasted for a few minutes.

It was Khe Sanh all over again. Garrett and Cameron were witnesses to the horror and got a taste of what Michael went through. In the morning Michael was shivering but recalled nothing of his response. It all got locked away again. Some of the shivering was partly from the sweating related to the flashbacks and partly from an ongoing condition that would come and go, which some doctors thought might be chronic malaria but never could be sure. His sons pulled out his warm robe from the closet, the robe he used whenever these shivering spells descended. They stayed with Michael that morning until all agreed Michael was secure and able to resume his daily life. But he never wanted his sons to ever have to relive or repeat to anyone what they saw and heard.

So, when is it over? Maybe Yogi really understood the truth.

NOTES

Chapter 2 THE NEIGHBORHOOD

1. Jamie Lerner, The Secret Behind Hell's Kitchen in All Its Filth and Glamour. April 8, 2121, distractify. com/p/why-is-hells-kitchen-called-that, 9
2. Ibid., 9
3. Ibid., 9

Chapter 6 THE LINE BETWEEN IS THIN

1. Gwen Draut, The Line Between is Thin, 2021, Short stories and poems

Chapter 11 SEVENTY-SEVEN DAYS

1. Jerry F. Limone, YOU DON'T KNOW, 1991
2. Newsweek, The Dusty Agony of Khe Sanh, March 18, 1968, 37
3. Ibid., 37
4. Ibid., 37
5. Ibid., 37

6. Time Magazine, How the Battle Of Khe Sanh Was Won, April 19, 1068, 30

7. Ibid., 30

8. Ibid., 31

9. Ibid., 31

10. Lt. Col Dave Grossman On Killing Boston: Little Brown& Company, 1995, 1996, 43-44

Printed in the United States
by Baker & Taylor Publisher Services